"Jing Gao's evocative debut cookbook embodies the author's tenacious, fearless spirit and unrelenting commitment to rewriting the narrative about the possibilities of modern Sichuan flavors. A delicious triumph."

—**HETTY LUI MCKINNON**, food writer and author of five cookbooks, including *To Asia, With Love* and *Tenderheart*

"Jing's *The Book of Sichuan Chili Crisp* is a coming-of-age story, a superb collection of recipes and food tales, and for me a very personal testament to the power of persistent entrepreneurial action. . . . There is so much of that wisdom in this book; you may not see it in the pickles or douban fish, in the hot pot or all the dumplings, but that's why they all taste so good. This book will change your life."

—**ANDREW ZIMMERN**, chef, writer, traveler, and TV host

"Jing Gao's Sichuan chili crisp is a reckoning. In her stunning, bold debut cookbook, we are invited into Jing's kitchen and her unique perspective on Sichuan flavors. This is more than just a cookbook; it's an ode to modern Chinese food, breaking away from the confines of tradition."

—**BETTY LIU**, author of *My Shanghai*

"Jing is not just a brilliant businessperson but a brilliant chef too. She has been teaching me how to cook her gorgeous, deeply personal Sichuan food for years via text and email—I think we are both extremely excited that I finally have this book to cook from instead. It is an absolute stunner."

—**NOAH GALUTEN**, chef, restaurateur, and author of *The Don't Panic Pantry Cookbook*

THE BOOK OF SICHUAN CHILI CRISP

THE BOOK OF SICHUAN CHILI CRISP

Spicy Recipes and Stories
from Fly By Jing's Kitchen

TEN SPEED PRESS
California | New York

To my grandparents,
who ignited my love for flavor

INTRODUCTION 1
THE SICHUAN PANTRY 19

Appetizers 35
Street Snacks 73
Main Courses 101
Vegetarian 141
Rice and Noodles 161
Sweets 183
Cocktails 201
Condiments
and Seasonings 215

ABOUT THE CONTRIBUTORS 232
ACKNOWLEDGMENTS 234
INDEX 236

INTRODUCTION

I remember the sweet, fiery chili oil dripping down my lips.

I was a little girl, growing up in Chengdu, the capital of China's Sichuan region. My parents and I would eat at fly restaurants—tiny, dingy, hole-in-the-wall places that are so good they're said to attract people like flies. At these popular spots, we'd grab bowls of Sichuan's best street food and homestyle cooking. The options were limitless: mung bean noodles, slippery wontons, and stewed pork belly topped with brown sugar. These places were nothing to look at, but the energy was unlike any. It was magical. And the flavors? Delicious, layered, and complex.

I didn't know it then, but those moments sitting crouched on a tiny plastic stool, eating bowls of hot noodles submerged in sweet chili oil were the most transformative of my life.

When I grew up and moved away from Chengdu, the food and memories from those fly restaurants stayed with me. My family relocated a lot—we lived in Germany, England, Austria, France, and Italy. My father was a nuclear physics professor with a Chinese visa, which meant he usually couldn't teach at one university for more than a year. Throughout grade school, I was always the new kid. I learned to adapt to my environment at a young age and adopted a Western name—Jenny—to try to appear less foreign, to blend in. Transience became the norm, and each year I had to learn a new culture and a new language—until finally, we settled in Canada for my high school years.

During all these moves, food brought me home. My mom would do her best to recreate memories of our favorite flavors, using ingredients she would find at the local European farmers' markets. They tasted of neither here nor there but were delicious nonetheless. We would occasionally go back to visit our family in Chengdu and return to the fly restaurants. There was something about the buzz of warmth from the sweet chili oil that reminded me of who I was.

I graduated from business school in Canada and went off into the corporate world. Around 2010, a job with a large tech company brought me back to Asia, where I lived in Beijing, Singapore, and Shanghai. It was exciting and intense, but I started to become undone. Who was I? Where was I from? What is my base? You could say I was having an identity crisis of sorts. The transience had caught up with me, and I had no firm ground to stand on.

Being in China forced me to realize how divorced I'd become from my roots all those years and how much I had pushed down and buried them, just to be seen, just to survive. I slowly peeled back the layers, and food gave me the courage to do so. In Beijing, I dug into the rich food culture of the capital, eating at the restaurants of provincial government offices known for most faithfully representing each region's cuisine. I studied with chefs and food historians and inquired about dishes. And to dive even deeper, I cooked.

It shocked me how wide and rich this 5,000-year-old culinary heritage actually was and how little of it was and is known outside the country. I saw how people came alive over food and witnessed the vibrant complexity of flavors from across the land. A perfect bowl of mapo tofu evoked tears. Chengdu's Zhong dumplings elicited smiles as wide as the entire country. A deceptively simple plate of pickles tasted anything but. There was life found in these layers of flavors, and more importantly, I uncovered layers of myself in between these bites.

I began to develop my own personal iterations of these complex Chinese flavors. I went on sourcing trips across the Sichuan countryside, learning the specificity of provenance and its impact on flavor and quality. Sichuan is known as the land of plenty, and for good reason. The climate and topography provide conditions for ingredients unmatched, creating flavors unparalleled. I created dishes that married flavors new and old. Everything was an evolution while being rooted in tradition—and I was finding my voice.

I started a popular blog on Chinese food and took celebrity chefs around the country to eat. Eventually, I found the courage to leave my day job and founded an award-winning fast-casual restaurant in Shanghai called Baoism. Whenever I could, I began hosting "underground" pop-up dinners around the world. I named these dinners, which I held everywhere from Hong Kong to Sydney to New York, Fly By Jing, a name pulled from my roots: an ode to the fly restaurants.

I loved how the layers of flavors in my dishes made me feel and how they made others light up. I often traveled to cook in places where people had never heard of these ingredients or tasted these flavors. Their reactions convinced me that appreciation for great flavor was universal, and there was a gap to be filled.

Everywhere I traveled, I kept with me a suitcase of meticulously sourced ingredients. I knew they were key to the flavors I cooked and could not be found anywhere else. I made big batches of sauces, spice mixes, and condiments of all kinds. Chili crisp, the versatile, spicy, umami-rich sauce was a base layer for many recipes as something to build up flavor, and it was something I took for granted. It was a pantry staple in Sichuan, and there were

thousands of variations across China, much like soy sauce and sesame oil. Recipes for chili crisp varied from family to family, passed down over generations. I began to concoct a personal blend, honoring my family's rendition while adding my own nuances. Guests at my dinners inquired about it, and I started bottling the stuff to give to friends and family. Demand grew, and I began selling it online and in local boutiques.

In 2018, I traveled to California to visit a natural food trade show called Expo West. Swimming through a sea of people over several days at the largest food exhibition in the country, I was struck by the lack of diversity in options. I could count on one hand the number of Asian food brands represented, and that didn't seem right, given how popular I knew these flavors were. I realized quickly that this was my opportunity. I launched Fly By Jing, my line of pantry staples featuring Sichuan chili crisp at its front and center, shortly thereafter via a crowdfunding campaign, and the rest, as they say, is history.

Today, everything I do revolves around flavor. It colors how I see the world and evokes memories and dreams of the future. The base of this flavor was and remains chili crisp. It punctuates my brand and all that I do. But chili crisp is also an invitation to feel and remember and be seen. The journey of building my company has helped me come home to myself. Along the way, I reclaimed my birth name, 婧 Jing.

This book is about this reclaiming. It tells the story of how I found—and continue to find—my identity through food. I am here because I have the utmost honor of being able to cook and explore the food of my home country. Sichuan chili crisp is the vessel through which I've been able to express my love for my culture. Fly By Jing's slogan "Not Traditional But Personal" speaks to the deeply meaningful pillars of heritage and the steadfast honoring of self, both of which is what I founded my brand on.

These pages also tell of the nuanced, layered, complicated, historical, and modern aspects of Chinese cuisines and the unparalleled magic of chili crisp. I say "magic" because it truly is just that. It can take any dish to the next level—from a traditional bowl of dan dan noodles (page 171) to your mother's favorite lemon cake. Chili crisp is meant to make you get in the kitchen and explore and experiment unfettered. It's meant to bring you closer to you.

My goal has always been to evolve culture through flavor. I want you to feel seen and heard when you cook and eat, just as I have done. Get curious. Get weird. Get bold.

Throughout all these years, the one truth I've learned and kept close is that flavor is a vehicle to tell our stories. When we're exposed to new sensations on our taste buds, we break barriers in ourselves and with others. That really is magic.

And so is sweet, fiery chili crisp dripping down your lips.

What is Sichuan Chili Crisp?

Like anything deeply personal, it's hard to describe chili crisp in one sentence. It's layered and nuanced. Crispy and spicy. Amorphous based on your interpretation. Something you feel on your tongue as much as you taste. Do you prefer more oil? More crunch? More savory, funky, sweet, or numbing? Make it yours. Chili crisp is the people's condiment: entirely democratic and entirely equalizing.

But then again, like anything deeply personal, it's inherently easy for me to talk about chili crisp because it's been at the core of my existence for this past decade.

Like me, chili crisp was born in China. A condiment made of electrifying spices and peppers, it's a marriage of texture and flavor and heat. Chili crisp provides the basis of a dish as much as it is a complement to it.

Like a true Sichuan local, I've added chili crisp to everything for as long as I can remember. I love its punch and mystery. I've always found Chinese chili sauces more complex and savory compared to their hot sauce counterparts in the West that tend to be acidic and can be one-dimensional. Discovering the sheer variation in styles and flavors of chili crisp has astounded me. In Guizhou province where the stalwart mass market brand Laoganma is made, a popular variant includes lacto-fermented chili peppers. In Sichuan, the leading flavor profile is often mala, or spicy and numbing. Elsewhere, you can find varieties with all manner of crunch from fried soybeans to nuts and seeds.

But it was always the homemade variations, packed with high-quality ingredients and without the fillers or flavor shortcuts that commercial ones contained, that tasted best. My family has never stocked any store-bought jars in the fridge, opting instead to craft their own, glistening red elixirs, slow cooked with aged, fermented fava bean paste, painstakingly sourced chilies, Sichuan pepper, and sometimes with homemade beef jerky and mushrooms mixed in. I took for granted that the flavors at home were always going to be more diverse and superior to something store-bought.

When I started cooking at my Shanghai restaurant, I really began to appreciate the specificity of ingredients. Not all chilies are made the same. Even within the same variety (of which there are thousands), there are numerous grades of quality—and that's just the chilies. That is why for a complex sauce with dozens of ingredients, it is often impossible to replicate the same flavors using ingredients sourced even a town away. In this way, chili crisp is the ultimate vessel for self-expression.

I started making my own chili crisp from scratch—for myself, my friends, and for the customers at my restaurant and pop-up supper clubs. I used the highest-quality erjingtiao chilies, known for their fragrance and luster, mountain-grown tribute peppers (so-called because they are so rare they were given exclusively as a tribute to the emperor), organic cold-pressed oils, and small-batch fermented black beans. I learned, too, that the element of time is also an ingredient, sometimes the most important one. The time and care it takes for preserved black beans to achieve their depth and their funk and the time it takes for all the elements to meld together after cooking are crucial elements in my chili crisp. I also added crunchy aromatics like golden-fried garlic and shallots, an influence from southern China, and mushroom and seaweed powders to add umami and depth of flavor without using common flavor shortcuts. You cannot fake the good stuff, and this was all good stuff.

Variations of oil-based chili sauces have evolved from cultures throughout the world, each holding its own heritage. Some of my favorites include bright Calabrian chili pastes from Italy, sambal oelek from Southeast Asia, and smoky salsa machas from Mexico. Each has its own draw and application, and I keep my pantry well stocked with all of them. The chili crisp I love most is the version we create at Fly By Jing that boasts a complex umami quality. It draws out the essence of Sichuan's best ingredients, while allowing their inherent flavors to shine.

As my sauces gained popularity, I was inspired to bring Sichuan flavors to the world and to shine light on the nuanced and complex roots of this culinary heritage. From the early days of launching a Kickstarter campaign to now selling in thousands of stores across the United States, and the often-excruciating path along the way, this humble sauce has carried my message far and wide. For me, chili crisp is far more than a condiment. It's a vessel that has carried forth my identity and has helped others find and honor theirs.

It's also the basis or inspiration for all the dishes I create in this book. These are recipes I've developed over many years and tables and stoves. Most of these have been served at countless pop-up dinners I've hosted. Each one weaves in an element of my past and present. They each tell my story—and, I hope, in many ways, they will help you tell yours.

WHAT IS SICHUAN CHILI CRISP?

THE SĪCHUAN PANTRY

When I was cooking pop-up dinners all over the world, I always had a suitcase packed with ingredients ready to go. My life was peripatetic. Much like my childhood, I was constantly adapting to an unfamiliar land, an unknown kitchen. But what was always familiar were the ingredients I brought with me from Sichuan. One of my favorite things to do in these many different places was to riff with collaborating chefs about incorporating Sichuan's intoxicating flavors into local produce, creating something as entirely new to our customers as they were to us.

The beauty of Sichuan's flavor profiles is that as complex as they are, they can be achieved with quite a limited number of ingredients, which I have listed below in order of importance. The quality of those ingredients is what matters and is what brings soul to a dish and integrity to the flavors. Like a firm handshake or steady eye contact, intention matters—and a dish's intention is bolstered by what it's made of.

Many of those ingredients that I spent years sourcing from the mountains and countryside of China had never been exported before, and when I started Fly By Jing, I wanted to make them more accessible to anyone craving the nostalgia or looking for a new experience. On our website, *www.flybyjing.com*, along with our initial line of sauces, we also sell the tribute peppers that I source from the mountains of Qingxi; the Pixian doubanjiang that is aged for several years, developing unimaginable umami along the way; and many more pantry essentials. These are key to making the deep flavors in these pages come alive. Look to Fly By Jing as your one-stop shop for where to buy the harder-to-find ingredients. For many other standard Chinese ingredients, you can find versions at your local Asian grocery store.

SICHUAN CHILI CRISP

No surprise here, Sichuan chili crisp is the most reached-for item in my pantry. I grew up eating this hot, savory, crispy, umami condiment drizzled over everything, and when I started making my own, I infused it with the ingredients I had sourced over the years in the Sichuan countryside, using techniques I had picked up from my family as well as from chefs I was lucky enough to learn from. What resulted was a singular expression of flavor, texture, and heat that I coined "not traditional, but personal," something I made for myself but have been honored to share with so many others. You can purchase my version or make your own (see page 220). Just know that the ingredients you source will express the flavor of your chili crisp in your own unique way. It is even likely that no two batches you make will taste the exact same, and that will forever be the beauty and ephemerality of chili crisp.

SICHUAN PEPPER

An ancient Chinese spice that has been cultivated in Sichuan for thousands of years, Sichuan pepper, or huajiao, is responsible for the cuisine's famous tongue-tingling sensation. Sichuan pepper is frequently mistaken for a type of chili pepper and incorrectly associated with capsicum's heat.

Made even more confusing by its name, Sichuan pepper is not even a peppercorn and holds no relation to it—it's actually the seed of a tree in the citrus family.

In recent years, Sichuan pepper has become more available in the United States, but like any other spice, it's prone to losing its flavor over time, especially if stored incorrectly. Many standard Sichuan peppers found on grocery store shelves have been collecting dust for years and are often a far cry from fresh high-quality versions. You can test your Sichuan pepper by placing one on your tongue and then chewing it. A good-quality one will light up your mouth with a powerful buzz and tingle. Depending on the strength of your Sichuan pepper, you may choose to adjust the quantities from what is called for in recipes. On Fly By Jing's website, we carry the freshest tribute peppers harvested every year in August, so you're guaranteed to have the most potent Sichuan pepper on hand at all times.

The best way to store your peppers is to keep them in the freezer, where their oils are preserved and can last more than a year. To use them, take out the quantity you need and heat them slowly in a pan on the stove to release their oils. This step coaxes out their optimal flavor and fragrance, but take care not to burn them. They can be sizzled with chilies in wok-fried dishes, thrown whole into braises, added to stir-fries and mapo tofu, or ground up and scattered on top of various dishes to add an extra dimension.

DRIED CHILI PEPPERS

Dried chili peppers are an essential part of Sichuan's cooking repertoire. The most popular variety called 二荆条 erjingtiao literally translates to "two strips of gold," referring to the way the chilies look on the vine. They are known for their mild spice but intense fragrance that doesn't overwhelm the taste of a dish but instead heightens sensations and awakens the palate to deeper flavors. Their uses are varied and inventive. They can be dry-fried in oil for a scorched-chili flavor, fermented with fava beans for Sichuan's famous doubanjiang, pickled to lend acidity to fish-fragrant sauce, ground up and combined with aromatics to create the canvas for the most fragrant chili oil, and mixed with various other spices to make dozens of Sichuan flavor profiles from mala (spicy and numbing) to guaiwei (strange flavor) that are a perfect balance of sweet, savory, spicy, sour, and numbing. You can find erjingtiao on Fly By Jing's website, but in a pinch, you can substitute with Mexican chiles de árbol. If you'd like extra heat, you can mix in some dried Thai bird's-eye chilies.

SICHUAN RAPESEED OIL

The first thing to get out of the way is that Sichuan's rapeseed oil is not the same as European rapeseed or canola oils, which have a decidedly bad rap for being highly processed seed oils. One of the most defining ingredients in Sichuan cooking is the fragrant, amber-hued caiziyou, a minimally processed oil from the seed of the manqing plant, also known as the field mustard *Brassica rapa* ssp. oleifera, which has been harvested in China since AD 300. In the nineteenth century, it was crossed with the European *Brassica napus* plant to produce a cultivar called 'Caiziyou', known in English as semi-winter rapa. Since then, the oil has been beloved in Sichuan cuisine for its nutty, fragrant, delicious flavor and is the star in all kinds of classic dishes and chili oils. The oil seeds are first toasted to develop their natural flavors, then cold-pressed and filtered to create a chili oil base like no other. Sichuan's caiziyou packs a deep flavor punch and numerous health benefits. It's naturally low in erucic acid, contains healthy omega-3 and -6 fatty acids, and is a great source of vitamin E.

SOY SAUCE

The Chinese have been brewing soy sauce since the thirteenth century, and it's one of the key seasonings to add savory flavor not just in the Sichuan pantry but also in many other Asian cuisines. There are many brands of soy sauces out there, from small-batch artisanal to mass-market produced, from regular to gluten free, seasoned to unseasoned, and aged to young. Chinese soy sauces typically use 100 percent soy and are brewed, while Japanese soy sauces are made from a combination of soy and wheat. There are further differences in those from Southeast Asia, which tend to be thicker and sweeter. I encourage you to try different varieties and find your favorite. The main thing to understand with Chinese soy sauce is the difference between light (shengchou) and dark (laochou) versions. When not specified, recipes in this book will call for light soy sauce, which has a bright, savory, and umami flavor. When specified, dark soy sauce is used to give a deeper richness and dark red color to dishes. It is thicker and syrupy, not as salty, and great when reduced in long braises and stir-fries.

BLACK VINEGAR

An essential ingredient for striking many of Sichuan's famously balanced flavor profiles, black vinegar is aromatic and umami-rich, acidic, and complex. It's made from rice and grains, fermented, and aged for several months or up to years at a time, much like balsamic vinegar. Like soy sauce, there are many varieties of black vinegar, with each region of China boasting its own methods and specialties. The eastern city of Zhenjiang, where my mother's family is from, is famous for their Zhenjiang vinegar, a version made with sticky rice. This is the most widespread version, and it is available in the Western world and will most likely be the one you'll find in your local Asian store. Sichuan also has a version called Baoning vinegar, made in northern Langzhong from wheat bran and a concoction of medicinal herbs. It's a bit mellower and has a slightly sweet finish. This is harder to find outside of China, but Zhenjiang vinegar is a great substitute and can be used for all recipes in this book. At Fly By Jing, we carry a ten-year-old aged version that is so smooth you could drink it. I use it for all my dishes that call for black vinegar, and it truly elevates every dish.

DOUBANJIANG

Often called the "soul" of Sichuan cooking, doubanjiang is made from fermented fava beans and erjingtiao chilies. It is at the heart of many of the province's signature dishes, providing heat, funk, and umami flavor to many classic dishes from mapo tofu (page 104) to twice-cooked pork (page 128). The best doubanjiang comes from a county called Pixian just outside of Chengdu, where factories have been fermenting their paste for hundreds of years. It's available in different levels of maturity; the most commercially available ones are less than one year old with a bright red

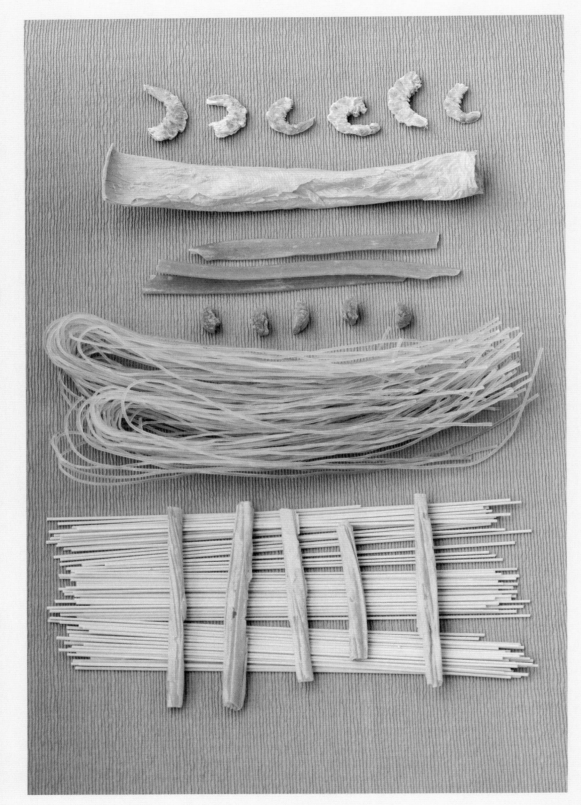

color. Less widely available are versions aged three years or more, where the flavor has developed to an incomparable depth, accompanied by a dark amber hue. At Fly By Jing, we carry a three-year-old aged doubanjiang that is one of the best in existence. It's made in a century-old factory that still ferments sauces the old-fashioned way in clay urns, building deep umami flavors slowly over time, completely naturally with no additives. I like to have both a younger and an aged version on hand at all times and often mix them together for recipes to achieve optimal flavor as well as color.

FERMENTED BLACK BEANS

Fermented black beans, also known as douchi, have a deep flavor similar to soy sauce and are made from soybeans steamed and then fermented for several months with salt and spices. Fermented black beans predate soy sauce and have been made in China for more than two thousand years. Much like the other pantry ingredients, there are many variations from regions all across China. In contrast to versions from Guangzhou that are drier and harder, Sichuan versions are plumper, softer, and extremely fragrant. They are an essential ingredient in my chili crisp, since they impart a depth hard to replicate with chilies and spices alone, and they add a chewy texture with each bite. They are also the basis for dishes calling for black bean flavor, many stir-fries, and mapo tofu (page 104).

SESAME OIL

Made from pressed, toasted sesame seeds, sesame oil's flavor and aroma are unmatched. It's widely used in Sichuan cooking as part of a dressing or as a dip and is added to heighten the aroma of hot dishes. Due to the volatility of its flavor compounds, sesame oil is usually added to dishes at the very end and not directly to the wok on high heat. Look for pure toasted sesame oil. It can be more expensive than those mixed with other oils, but a little goes a long way, so a small bottle will last you a while.

SESAME PASTE

Chinese sesame paste, an essential ingredient in dressings and cold dishes, is quite different from tahini in both texture and flavor. It's made from deeply toasted sesame seeds rather than untoasted or lightly toasted seeds and has an intoxicating fragrance and incredible nuttiness. In a pinch, you can substitute with tahini, which is usually made with untoasted sesame seeds and is much more readily available in the United States.

YIBIN YACAI

It's hard to put into words the magic of yacai, an aromatic, crunchy, sweet, and savory condiment made from the pickled stems of a type of mustard green. A specialty from the city of Yibin in Sichuan, these mustard stems are sun-dried and salted, left to ferment for several months and then packed into clay jars with brown sugar and spices for a second fermentation. It can be a bit difficult to find yacai; it is often sold in small airtight packages in the pickle section of Chinese markets. Yacai is essential in Sichuan classics like dan dan noodles (page 171) and ants climbing up a tree (page 120), adding an unmistakable savory depth and crunchy mouthfeel.

PICKLED MUSTARD GREENS

There are numerous varieties of pickles made from Chinese leafy green mustards from regions across China, but the one most commonly found in Sichuan cuisine is a variety called suancai, made with large petiole mustard greens lacto-fermented in a spiced salt brine. Suancai adds a sour, salty flavor that is delicious when chopped and added to stir-fries, soups, or fish dishes. You can readily find it in Asian markets, packed in brine inside a vacuum-sealed bag.

ROCK SUGAR

Rock sugar, made from boiling sugar cane and letting the liquid crystallize, is an essential Chinese sweetener that departs a gentler, more mellow sweetness than granulated sugar. It's used to balance out savory or acidic flavors and departs an alluring, high-shine gloss when reduced in a sauce on dishes such as red-braised pork belly (page 123), deviled tea eggs (page 57), and spicy scallion oil noodles (page 177). The crystals can sometimes be quite large, but you can easily break down a larger piece by smashing it on a cutting board with the flat side of a cleaver. Most Chinese cooks just measure rock sugar by eye, throwing in a small or large chunk, based on how much sweetness a dish calls for. Since rock sugar is not super sweet, inconsistent amounts can be more forgiving.

FURU (FERMENTED TOFU)

Fermented tofu is one of those ingredients that probably scares away most people who aren't familiar with it, in a similar way that Vegemite or a ripe blue cheese might. But for those who know it, they love it for the deep, savory funk that only furu can impart, whether used as a topping for congee, a dipping sauce for hot pot, or when mixed with sesame paste, soy sauce, vinegar, and sugar for a shockingly addictive sauce (see page 228) that can make hand-pulled noodles or stir-fried leafy greens pop. Furu is made by fermenting fresh tofu in water, salt, and rice wine and is usually sold as cubes packed in jars of water or oil. It comes in countless variations, including a red version colored with red yeasted rice, a rose-flavor version from Yunnan, and my personal favorite from Sichuan, flavored with—you guessed it—chili oil and spices.

DRY SPICES

A wide array of spices and herbs is in the arsenal of every Sichuan kitchen and is essential for adding the fragrance and complexity that the cuisine is known for. A visit to a spice market in Chengdu is an experience for all the senses, with rows and rows of perfectly formed piles of spices of all shapes and colors. There are hundreds of herbs and dry spices available to concoct stewed meats, hot pots, and other dishes, but to keep it simple, the most frequently used ones in my pantry are star anise, an eight-pointed star with a deep anise fragrance, and cassia bark, the dried bark of the cassia tree that is evocative of cinnamon.

SĪCHUAN:
The Land of Plenty

For thousands of years, China's Sichuan Province was known as the land of plenty (天府之国 tianfuzhiguo). Its warm and wet climate and a terrain rich in rivers and fertile plains created agricultural abundance. Its cuisine is known throughout China and the world for its mind-blowing spice and heat, but its depth and complexity are often underestimated.

Chengdu, the capital, and the city where I was born, sits in the Sichuan basin, surrounded by mountains with the Qinghai-Tibetan Plateau to its west. The topography made getting to the city so difficult that Tang dynasty poet Li Bai described a journey there as "more difficult than the road to heaven." Still, Sichuan Province was and remains a destination. Dynastic upheavals over the last thousand years have drawn waves of immigrants, bringing fresh culinary and cultural customs.

Like most living and breathing culinary cultures, it's hard to pin down what exactly Sichuan food is. It's ever evolving and all the better for it. Located along the Silk Road and the Tea Horse Road, major trade routes to the West, Sichuan also absorbed many outside influences into its culture and culinary practices. Most notable among them was the adoption of chili peppers from South America and cooking techniques from northern and eastern parts of China. Heat and spice are such a dominant feature of the cuisine today that it's hard to fathom that chilies only arrived in China less than three hundred years ago. This blending of old and new ideas has made Sichuan food one of the original fusion cuisines.

The Sichuan people's love of spice can be attributed to the region's muggy climate. According to principles of traditional Chinese medicine, dampness creates imbalance in the body and can be driven out by eating foods that are "heating" in nature. In the early days, the heat came not from chilies but from a combination of ginger, Sichuan pepper, and cornel berries, the ruby-red fruit of the Cornus mas plant. These aromatics comprise the 辛辣 xin la, or pungent spice flavor, that is valued by Sichuan chefs over pure, fiery heat. In the seventeenth century, when chili peppers arrived, the locals were quick to adopt chilies. They discovered their perfect harmony with the aromatic numbing sensation of Sichuan pepper, and the chili quickly became an integral part of the cuisine.

Sichuan pepper, an ancient Chinese spice that has been cultivated in Sichuan for thousands of years, is responsible for the cuisine's famous tongue-tingling sensation. Despite its colloquial name, it's actually the seed of a tree in the citrus family and isn't related to the common peppercorn. There are dozens of varieties in China, and just like the finest wine grapes and coffee beans, climate and terroir play a big part in expressing its characteristics. The most famous and coveted are grown in Hanyuan County outside of Chengdu, in a mountainous village called Qingxi, which sits along the Tea Horse Road. These were so prized for their many medicinal and culinary uses that they were offered exclusively as a tribute to the emperor, hence their name tribute pepper, or 贡椒 gongjiao.

Some of my favorite ingredient sourcing trips were to Qingxi every August during harvest season. The heady fragrance of ripened tribute peppers in the misty mountain air is something extraordinary—citrusy, deep, and layered. The fragrance permeates your skin and lingers on your clothing for days to come. In fact, the spice was used as a fragrance before it was used in cooking. The delicate kernels are painstakingly hand-harvested in small quantities and sell out almost immediately, so it pays to show up in person. Thrown whole into long braises and stews or roasted and ground to top iconic dishes like mapo tofu and twice-cooked pork, just-harvested tribute peppers can be transformational. It's even believed that the reason for their widespread use in Sichuan cuisine is because they numb the senses to allow ever more consumption of chilies!

Not all the region's flavor profiles are spicy. Sichuan's chefs are renowned for their ability to combine very few ingredients to create over twenty-four taste combinations known as compound flavors, or fuhewei, each with its distinct characteristics. Of these, only a handful feature the spiciness famously associated with Sichuan cuisine. Examples of flavor profiles lesser known but just as iconic include jiaoyan weixing (salt and Sichuan pepper flavor), a deceptively simple combination of roasted ground Sichuan pepper and salt that is inventively applied on everything from fried chicken to freshly baked walnut cookies. There's also lychee flavor, which contains no lychees but combines sweet and sour notes in imitation of the fruit and is applied to a savory canvas like fried pork over rice. Similarly, fish-fragrant flavor is a bold combination of pickled chili, vinegar, sugar, ginger, garlic, and scallions that has little to do with fish but evokes tastes of fish dishes that are sometimes dressed in a similar sauce. What unifies all twenty-four flavors are their precise balance and a complex umami or xian quality. Rather than overshadowing the natural taste of raw ingredients, it instead delicately draws out their essence.

39   Sichuan Lacto-Fermented Pickles

41   Celtuce, Vermicelli, and Chicken Salad

45   Celtuce in Tribute Pepper Oil

46   Cucumber and Yuba Salad

49   Leek, Tofu, and Peanut Salad

50   Yuzu Tribute Pepper Crudo

53   Strange-Flavor Poke

        53 Pickled Red Onions

54   Chilled Tofu with Avocado

57   Deviled Tea Eggs

58   Silky Steamed Eggs

61   Chengdu Scallion Pancakes

62   Saliva Chicken

APPETĪZERS

SICHUAN LACTO-FERMENTED PICKLES

Pickled vegetables are fundamental to Sichuan cooking, and when eaten along with rice, they are arguably the most important part of a meal. The pride of every Sichuan household is its collection of 泡菜坛子 paocaitanzi, handmade earthenware urns or crocks with a trough around their necks that act as a water seal for the lids. Its dark environment fosters the perfect conditions for lacto-fermentation. The vegetables emerge from the urns naturally crunchy, acidic, and distinctly flavored with Sichuan rice wine, ginger, cassia bark, star anise, Sichuan pepper, and chili.

Pickling brine can be decades old, passed down by the matriarchs of the family, with each generation adding its own signature to the flavor. Different crocks serve different purposes. Some are used to hold "old pickles," like the long-fermented mustard leaves used in the broth for 酸菜鱼 suancaiyu (pickled mustard green fish; page 108). Others are used for only a short period for pickles left just overnight; this is particularly the case with vegetables that have a high water content, like cucumbers, celtuce, and small radishes, giving them the name "shower pickles," since they merely take a quick dip in the brine.

Often served as a free appetizer in most restaurants, it's not uncommon to judge an establishment based on the quality of its pickles or a household on the cleanliness of its crock. Despite the simple ingredients and process, consistently perfect pickles are remarkably difficult to produce. Some claim that only the water and climate in Sichuan produce the right conditions for pickling, and I tend to agree. My pickling brine in Shanghai, where it's very humid, almost always found a way to spoil, and the pickles never quite had the exact same punch as those in my crocks in Chengdu. I even visited the self-proclaimed Sichuan pickle capital that hosts hundreds of factories slowly fermenting vegetables in giant crocks underground. They supply most of the commercially made ready-to-eat Sichuan pickles in China. The town square has a giant 18-foot statue of a pickling crock, and there's even a museum dedicated to the art of traditional pickling. Needless to say, we take our pickles seriously.

Like much else in Sichuan's food culture, pickling is an art and tradition that are steadfastly preserved, protected, and celebrated. As the Chinese saying goes, 民以食为天 minyishiweitian, "to the people, food is heaven."

Pickles are one of the first things I learned to make from my family in Sichuan, and nothing reminds me more of home. The hardest part about making these at home will be getting the right pickling crock and making sure it's stored and attended to properly. It may not taste exactly like what you'll find in Chengdu, but you can come pretty darn close, especially if you're using those elusive tribute peppers in your pickling brine.

CONTINUED

Search for a 4-quart ceramic or clay crock with thick walls that are insulated and that don't expose your pickles to light (glass crocks are not ideal here), preferably with a moat around the mouth that you can line with water to allow gas to escape and prevent oxygen from entering. When ready, the pickles will have a deep lacto-fermented flavor tinged with the citrusy numbing of tribute peppers and layers of warm flavor from the chilies, ginger, garlic, and spices. Serve with a drizzle of chili oil. *Makes 20 servings*

8 cups / 1.9L water,
　or as needed
¾ cup / 150g sea salt
1 or 2 pieces rock sugar
　(about 1 oz / 30g)
¼ cup / 60ml Chinese
　grain liquor or vodka
1 or 2 large pieces
　ginger (about 75g),
　sliced
2 or 3 erjingtiao chilies
1 Tbsp Sichuan pepper

PICKLING VEGETABLES OF
YOUR CHOICE:
2 or 3 carrots, cut into
　shape of your choice
1 daikon, cut into shape
　of your choice
½ head cabbage, cut into
　2-inch / 5cm pieces
1 bunch long string
　beans
2 to 3 pieces fresh red
　and green chilies

Chili oil for drizzling
　(optional)

1　In a large pot over high heat, add the water, salt, and rock sugar, and bring to a boil, ensuring both the salt and sugar are dissolved. Remove the pot from the heat and let the brine cool to room temperature.

2　Working with clean hands, pour the brine into a clean crock and add the alcohol, ginger, chilies, and Sichuan pepper. Add the vegetables to the crock, ensuring all are submerged under the liquid. Cover the crock, fill the trough of the vessel with water, and place in a cool, shady place, such as under your kitchen sink, for about 2 weeks. Fill the moat with water and check on it every few days. You'll need to refill the water in the trough and open the jar to let the gas release. Every time you touch the crock or take out any vegetables inside, make sure to wash your hands thoroughly and use very clean chopsticks or tongs; otherwise, the pickling brine can easily spoil. You'll know it's happy when you hear regular farts coming from the jar.

3　After 2 weeks, they should taste salty, tart, and crunchy, use very clean chopsticks or gloved hands to reach into the crock and take out what you'd like to use. To serve, chop into bite-sized pieces and drizzle with the chili oil, if you wish.

4　You can keep the remainder of the pickles in the crock and enjoy them over several weeks. You'll know when the pickles are too "old," once they begin to taste very sour. After the existing vegetables have been depleted, you can add more vegetables to the crock, keeping the same pickling liquid.

CELTUCE, VERMICELLI, AND CHICKEN SALAD

This is an adaptation of a dish that perhaps holds more meaning for me than any other in the world: my grandfather's rabbit salad. Some of my earliest food memories were made eating around the dining table in my grandparents' kitchen in Guanghan, the small town outside of Chengdu where I was born. The dish that always stood out to me was the "red rabbit" salad, a glistening concoction of vermicelli, leek, lightly pickled celtuce, and hand-shredded cured rabbit meat. This dish is deceptively simple but astounds with its balanced spicy, savory, acidic, sweet, and tingly profile, alongside the textures of roasted rabbit, vibrant crunch of the celtuce, and slipperiness of the vermicelli. The leek cuts into the strong flavors with a kick as well.

Because of the warm and wet climate of Sichuan and its fertile, grassy plains, there are a lot of rabbits, and people love eating their tasty and lean meat. If you've been to Chengdu, you've probably seen the endless shops selling rabbit head and stewed rabbit meats. "Red rabbit" 红兔, however, is a hyperlocal specialty from Guanghan that most people in Chengdu have never even heard of.

"Red rabbit" is made by hanging the meat to cure, after it's been rubbed in a mixture of its own blood and spices (hence the name), and then stewed in a rich and aromatic broth that gives it a deeply infused flavor and bouncy texture. You can buy it from specialty vendors in Guanghan (it's definitely not something you attempt at home) and eat it chopped up and steamed or in our family's preferred method of preparation as a cold appetizer.

Try as I might to smuggle red rabbit meat in my suitcase, I always lose to TSA in that battle, so I've had to adapt the recipe over the years when I'm outside of Sichuan. I usually opt for poached or roasted chicken meat. You can also substitute confit rabbit meat for a version even more true to the original. *Makes 4 servings*

Kosher salt for boiling and sprinkling
1 (½-inch / 1cm) slice ginger
⅓ cup / 50g leek, white part only, cut into 3-inch / 7.5cm segments and thinly sliced
½ lb / 225g chicken breast or thigh meat
8 oz / 225g celtuce (1 or 2 stalks)
6 oz / 170g vermicelli

1 Fill a medium pot halfway and bring the water to a boil over high heat, then salt the water liberally and add the ginger and leek. Lower the heat to low, add the chicken, cover the pot, and cook for 10 to 15 minutes, until the chicken reaches an internal temperature of 165°F / 75°C on an instant-read thermometer and the middle of the meat is opaque. Remove the chicken from the pot and let cool. Once cool, use your hands or a fork to shred the chicken. Place in a bowl and set aside.

2 To prepare the celtuce: Using a cleaver, chop the celtuce into 3-inch / 7.5cm segments, then chop off the thick outer skin to reveal its jade-colored flesh. Julienne the celtuce evenly to a ⅛-inch / 3mm thickness. (I like to use a mandoline first to achieve even sheets before stacking them and cutting into batons.)

DRESSING

3 Tbsp Sichuan Chili
Crisp (page 220),
or as needed

2 Tbsp soy sauce

2 Tbsp black vinegar

2 tsp granulated
sugar

Dash of toasted
sesame oil

Dash of Ground
Roasted Sichuan
Pepper (page 218),
or as needed

Chopped cilantro
leaves for garnish

3 Place the celtuce in a large bowl and sprinkle it with
about 2 tsp kosher salt. Using your hands, massage
the salt all over and let the celtuce sweat for about
10 minutes to lightly pickle. Drain the excess water
that has been expelled. The celtuce should taste lightly
salted and crunchy and should have lost its raw flavor.

4 Cook the vermicelli according to the package
instructions. Drain and set aside.

5 To make the dressing: In a small bowl, mix the chili crisp,
soy sauce, vinegar, sugar, sesame oil, and roasted
Sichuan pepper together.

6 In a large bowl, combine the vermicelli, celtuce, shredded
chicken, and leek. Pour the dressing over the mixture and
adjust to taste. You can add more chili crisp or Sichuan
pepper, depending on the freshness and potency of your
variety. Garnish with the cilantro.

CELTUCE IN TRIBUTE PEPPER OIL

Celtuce, a humble Chinese vegetable that features heavily in Sichuan home cooking, has steadily gained popularity in the United States, even popping up on fine dining menus as chefs like Dan Barber, formerly at Blue Hill at Stone Barns, discovered its refreshingly nutty flavor and cucumber-like texture. I'm personally thrilled by this, since it means I can now get one of my favorite vegetables at most Asian grocery stores, whenever I want.

A type of stem lettuce, celtuce is usually harvested for its stem, even though the leaves are also edible. In Sichuan, the preparations for celtuce are numerous; they're used in stir-fries and soups and are sometimes served pickled or even raw. You'll find them in season from late spring to early summer. Look for celtuce with thick, smooth stalks (you'll be peeling off a lot of its hard skin) and look at the base of the stem to check that it doesn't have a hollow center, as that would indicate it's old.

My favorite way to prepare celtuce is also the easiest way. Quick-pickled with some salt, just enough to get rid of its raw flavor, it becomes lightly seasoned and crunchy. It's the perfect canvas for a fragrant dressing like Tribute Pepper Oil that allows its delicate flavors to still shine through. _Makes 4 servings_

1 lb / 450g celtuce
(about 2 stalks)
2 tsp kosher salt

DRESSING
1 Tbsp toasted
sesame oil
1 tsp Tribute Pepper Oil
(page 219)
2 tsp unseasoned
rice vinegar
½ tsp agave or honey
1 tsp kosher salt

1 scallion, green part
only, thinly sliced,
for garnish

1 To prepare the celtuce: Using a cleaver, chop the celtuce into 3-inch / 7.5cm segments, then chop off the thick outer skin to reveal its jade-colored flesh. Julienne the celtuce evenly to a ⅛-inch / 3mm thickness. I like to use a mandoline first to achieve even sheets before stacking them and cutting into batons.

2 Place the celtuce in a large bowl and sprinkle it with the salt. Using your hands, massage the salt all over and let the celtuce sweat for about 10 minutes to lightly pickle. Drain the excess water that has been expelled. The celtuce should taste lightly salted and crunchy and should have lost its raw flavor.

3 To make the dressing: In a small bowl, mix the sesame oil, tribute pepper oil, vinegar, agave, and salt together. Pour the dressing over the celtuce and toss to coat.

4 Serve the celtuce in your dish of choice and garnish with the scallions.

CUCUMBER AND YUBA SALAD

This is a variation of a commonly found appetizer in Chinese restaurants, the simple smashed cucumber salad. While it's refreshing, the dish can sometimes be one dimensional and a little boring, so I like to add layers to keep things interesting. One of my favorite textural contrasts to add to the crunchy cucumbers are the slippery layers of yuba, or tofu skin. Since they work really great together they have subsequently become one of my go-to-appetizers on a hot summer day. You can usually buy dried yuba in sheets that are ready to be rehydrated. *Makes 4 servings*

¾ cup / 140g dried yuba sheets or sticks, cut into 1-inch / 2.5cm pieces
2 large cucumbers
¼ tsp kosher salt
¼ tsp granulated sugar

SAUCE
1 Tbsp Sichuan Chili Crisp (page 220)
1 Tbsp soy sauce
1 Tbsp black vinegar
1 tsp granulated sugar
2 tsp toasted sesame oil
1 Tbsp minced garlic

1 tsp sesame seeds for garnish
Chopped cilantro leaves for garnish

1   Fill a medium pot halfway and bring the water to a boil over high heat. Add the yuba and cook for 4 to 5 minutes, until the yuba turns from yellow to white and has a soft texture. Drain and set aside.

2   Halve the cucumbers and then quarter them. Cut the quarters into segments about 3 inches / 7.5cm long. Using the flat side of a cleaver, smash down on the cucumbers to crack the outside skin. Remove the seeds and discard. Cut the cucumbers into bite-sized pieces.

3   Place the cucumbers in a medium bowl and add the salt and sugar. Mix well to combine and let sit for at least 30 minutes. You will see liquid from the cucumbers being expelled during this time.

4   When ready to serve, drain the cucumbers of excess water. In a large bowl, combine the cucumbers with the yuba. Add the chili crisp, soy sauce, vinegar, sugar, sesame oil, and garlic, and toss well to combine. Garnish with the sesame seeds and cilantro.

LEEK, TOFU, AND PEANUT SALAD

I first had a version of this dish in Chengdu at a "private kitchen," one of the popular underground supper clubs that have emerged as the new, more haute version of fly restaurants. I was struck by its simplicity—it's a three-ingredient dish that comes together to form a sum greater than its parts. This is an exploration of textures: the slipperiness of just barely cooked leeks shines against firm, smoky, and seasoned tofu and the crunch of fried peanuts. All of it is tied together with a punchy sweet, savory, and acidic chili crisp vinaigrette. I love making this for dinner parties because you can prepare it way in advance. The flavors meld together even better after it's been sitting for a few hours. You can buy seasoned, pressed tofu in vacuum-sealed bags in the tofu section of your Asian grocery store. It is usually square-shaped and brown in color, having been braised and caramelized in soy sauce and spices. It's great in this salad, stir fries, or just sliced and eaten as a snack like hard cheese. _Makes 4 servings_

3 Tbsp vegetable oil
2 or 3 long leeks, white parts only, sliced into 1-inch / 2.5cm rounds
1 tsp kosher salt
8 oz / 230g seasoned or soy sauce braised pressed tofu, cut into 1-inch / 2.5cm cubes
½ cup / 120ml Chili Crisp Vinaigrette (page 226)
1 tsp roasted sesame seeds
½ cup / 30g store-bought fried peanuts
Chopped cilantro leaves for garnish

1   In a medium nonstick pan over medium heat, warm 2 Tbsp of the oil over medium heat. Add the leeks and ½ tsp of the salt and stir-fry for about 3 minutes, until the leeks are starting to cook but still retain their shape and are not too translucent and soft. Remove the pan from the heat, transfer to a large bowl, and let cool.

2   Heat the remaining 1 Tbsp of the oil in the same pan over medium heat. Add the tofu cubes and the remaining ½ tsp salt and stir-fry for 3 to 4 minutes total, until the tofu is lightly seared on each side. Remove the pan from the heat and let cool.

3   Add the cooled tofu cubes to the bowl with the leeks. Pour in the vinaigrette, add the sesame seeds, and mix well to combine. Marinate for an hour at room temperature or overnight in the refrigerator.

4   When ready to serve, toss with the peanuts, transfer to a serving platter, and garnish with the cilantro.

YUZU TRIBUTE PEPPER CRUDO

This hamachi (yellowtail) crudo appetizer is simple to prepare, packs a punch, and highlights the flavors of the tribute pepper oil and yuzu ponzu. You can use salmon, tuna, halibut, or any other sashimi-grade fish to prepare this, but hamachi is one of my favorites because of its rich, buttery texture. Yuzu ponzu is available at most Asian grocery stores, but if you can't find it, you can substitute it with a 1:2 ratio of soy sauce and yuzu or lemon juice. The tribute pepper oil in this recipe is key. It adds a bright and citrusy zing that will make your lips tingle and is a perfect pairing with the yuzu ponzu. We make a premium tribute pepper oil at Fly By Jing, but you can also make your own if you have access to high-quality Sichuan pepper.

Makes 4 servings

7 oz / 200g hamachi

SAUCE
3 Tbsp yuzu ponzu
1 tsp Tribute Pepper Oil
  (page 219)
1 tsp toasted sesame oil

GARNISH CHOICES
Salmon roe
Thinly sliced serrano or
  red chili pepper
Microgreens (such as
  cilantro or edible
  flowers)
Roasted sesame seeds
Chili Oil (page 219)

Flaky salt (such as
  Maldon)

1   Place the hamachi in the freezer for about 5 minutes, while you prepare the sauce and garnishes. You want the flesh to firm up a bit to make it easier to slice cleanly.

2   To make the sauce: In a small bowl, mix the ponzu, tribute pepper oil, and sesame oil together. Set aside.

3   To prepare the fish: Cut the hamachi into slices about ⅕ inch / 0.5cm in thickness and arrange on a large plate with tall edges. Pour the sauce over the fish and place your choice of garnish on top. I love the extra umami and pop of salmon roe and the heat of thinly sliced chili pepper. If you want to turn up the heat even more, add dots of red chili oil for vibrancy and heat. Finish with a sprinkling of flaky salt.

STRANGE-FLAVOR POKE

Strange flavor is one of Sichuan's famous twenty-four iconic flavors that linger on your mind and taste buds. Complex and balanced, it works when drizzled on almost any canvas. It is so named because of the strangely alluring blend of sweet, spicy, savory, nutty, and tingly elements. You can't put your finger on what exactly it is, but somehow everything works in unison. To me, strange flavor is magic. I love to pour it over any protein like shredded chicken breast, crispy tofu, or raw fish, as shown in this recipe, but you can really add it to anything you like. That's its beauty. Lettuce cups are a delightful base for this poke, but you can also serve it over rice. _Makes 4 servings_

1 lb / 450g sushi-grade
   fish (such as tuna
   or salmon), diced into
   bite-sized chunks
½ cup Strange-Flavor
   Sauce (page 227)
1 head butter lettuce

TOPPINGS
Roasted sesame seeds
Crushed peanuts
Chopped cilantro leaves
Pickled Red Onions
   (recipe follows)

1 In a large bowl, toss the fish chunks with the sauce.

2 When ready to serve, portion out roughly 2 Tbsp for each lettuce cup and finish with your desired toppings.

PICKLED RED ONIONS

This is a great staple to always have on hand in your fridge. It adds a perfect acidity and brightness to most dishes. Use a mandoline for uniform, thin slices. _Makes 2 cups_

1 Tbsp granulated sugar
1 tsp kosher salt
1 cup / 240ml water
½ cup / 120ml unseasoned rice
   vinegar, white wine vinegar,
   or apple cider vinegar
1 red onion, thinly sliced

In a small saucepan over medium heat, add the sugar, salt, water, and vinegar and mix until everything dissolves, about 3 minutes. Once done, remove the saucepan from the heat and cool the liquid, about 15 minutes.

Place the onions in a jar with an airtight lid and pour the cooled-down liquid over them. Store in the refrigerator for up to 1 month.

CHILLED TOFU WITH AVOCADO

This is probably one of the easiest recipes in the book and is also one of the most rewarding ones. It requires no cooking and comes together in minutes, especially if you've premade the chili crisp vinaigrette. We've all been there—you're hungry, tired, and just want to whip something together quickly but not sacrifice flavor or your health. I always keep a block of soft tofu in the fridge for this reason. The acidity of the vinaigrette is cut by the bright, citrusy flavor of the shiso leaf, and the creaminess of the avocado offers a textural complement to the melt-in-your-mouth silken tofu. It's hard to believe a dish this tasty can come together in less than five minutes. _Makes 4 servings_

1 lb / 450g silken tofu
½ avocado, peeled
¼ cup / 60ml Chili Crisp
  Vinaigrette (page 226)
½ tsp minced ginger
4 pieces shiso or perilla
  leaf, thinly sliced
1 tsp roasted sesame
  seeds
1 tsp store-bought fried
  shallots

1   Open the package of tofu and pour out any excess water. Place a few paper towels over the package and turn the tofu upside down onto the paper towels for a few minutes to ensure all water is soaked up. Remove the paper towels and gently slide the tofu onto a serving plate in one piece.

2   Cut the avocado into thin slices lengthwise, keeping one end intact. Fan out the avocado slices with a knife and transfer to the top of the tofu.

3   Pour the chili vinaigrette over the tofu, top with the ginger, shiso leaf, sesame seeds, and shallots. Serve immediately.

DEVILED TEA EGGS

I love eggs in all forms: scrambled, fried, boiled, steamed, or baked. I love them all. But my favorite egg preparation has got to be tea eggs, hard-boiled eggs steeped for hours in an aromatic stew of soy sauce, black tea, rock sugar, and spices. When I was growing up, my mom would often make a huge pot of tea eggs for me to snack on throughout the week. Later, when I lived in China as an adult, I would frequent convenience stores and street vendors who inevitably had an electric rice cooker filled with hard-boiled eggs simmering gently in a fragrant black broth. I probably ate one or two every single day, and they never got old. This recipe is a fun way to combine the complex flavors of tea eggs with a party-friendly finger food and is sure to impress. The mala spice mix addition to the yolk mixture adds an extra kick.
Makes 6 servings

12 eggs
⅔ cup / 160ml light
   soy sauce
2 Tbsp dark soy sauce
1 tsp granulated sugar
   or 1 small piece
   rock sugar
2 pieces star anise
2 Tbsp black tea
1 piece cassia bark
1 whole Sichuan pepper

1 tsp Dijon mustard
¼ cup / 60g mayonnaise
1 Tbsp minced shallot or
   onion
1 tsp Mala Spice Mix
   (page 223)
Kosher salt and ground
   black pepper for
   seasoning
2 or 3 scallions, green
   parts only, thinly
   sliced, for garnish

1. Place the eggs in a single layer in a large pot and fill with enough water to cover. Place the pot over high heat and bring the water to a boil. Lower the heat to medium and let the eggs cook for 5 minutes.

2. Meanwhile, prepare an ice bath.

3. When the 5 minutes are up, using a slotted spoon, remove the eggs (leave the hot water in the pot) and submerge them in the prepared ice bath to chill for a few minutes. Then, using the back of a spoon, gently tap the eggs to crack the shells all over, without breaking them. You can also just take the egg and tap it against a hard surface like a cutting board. The design gets more interesting the more you tap, so get creative.

4. Return the eggs to the pot with the hot water. Add both soy sauces, the sugar, star anise, tea, cassia bark, and Sichuan pepper. Bring to a boil, then turn down the heat to the lowest setting and let the eggs simmer slowly for about an hour. Remove the pot from the heat and let the eggs steep further overnight.

5. These eggs will be delicious enough to eat as is, but if you're feeling fancy or need something to impress at your next potluck, you can now turn these into deviled eggs. Slice the eggs in half lengthwise. Remove the yolks and place them in a medium bowl; set the egg whites aside. Using a fork, mash the yolks. Add the mustard, mayonnaise, shallot, spice mix, and salt and black pepper to taste.

6. Using a piping bag, pipe the yolk into the emptied egg white halves and sprinkle with scallions to serve.

SILKY STEAMED EGGS

There are few textures I love more in this world than the silken mouthfeel of freshly made tofu or the soft jiggle of barely set steamed eggs. The latter are easier to make at home and come together in just minutes. In their simplest variation, eggs are beaten, mixed with water, and steamed until set. Homestyle versions popular in Sichuan are finished with a drizzle of sesame oil, soy sauce, and fragrant fried minced pork. I'm partial to the salty pop of salmon roe with soy sauce and a drizzle of chili oil as a topping, but you can really dress them however you want. I once learned from a Japanese chef to mix the beaten egg with stock or dashi instead of water and to pass it through a fine-mesh strainer before steaming to ensure the smoothest texture and umami-rich flavor. I haven't looked back since. _Makes 4 servings_

2 eggs
1⅓ cups / 315ml dashi
    or vegetable stock
1 Tbsp mirin
1 Tbsp soy sauce, plus
    more for topping
1½ oz / 40g salmon
    roe for topping
Chili Oil (page 219)
    for topping

1   Using a whisk, beat the eggs in a medium bowl. Add the dashi, mirin, and soy sauce and whisk well. Strain through a fine-mesh sieve into a bowl or pitcher with a spout and discard any chunky bits. Divide the egg mixture among four ramekins or small bowls and cover each one securely with plastic wrap.

2   In a pot fitted with a steamer basket over medium-low heat, bring 1 to 2 inches / 2.5 to 5cm water to a simmer. Place the ramekins in the steamer basket, cover the pot, and cook until the eggs are set, about 15 minutes.

3   Remove the ramekins from the pot and take off the plastic wrap. Top the steamed eggs with the roe, soy sauce, and chili oil. Serve hot.

CHENGDU SCALLION PANCAKES

There's something universally appealing about a crispy fried dough. Whether it's a paratha, roti, or, in this case, a scallion pancake, these quick and deliciously flaky snacks can bring a bit of warm, crunchy magic to help you power through your midday slump or midnight hunger pangs. This recipe is a twist on the classic scallion pancake and is flavored with mala spice mix, a potent blend of herbs and spices that brings a warming heat and flavor intrigue that perfectly balances the crispy, flaky pancakes. When served as an appetizer with a dip of soy sauce and Sichuan chili crisp, they'll be the first to go at a dinner party. _Makes 4 servings_

2 cups / 250g
 all-purpose flour,
 or as needed
⅔ cup / 160ml hot water,
 or as needed
2 Tbsp lard or coconut oil
2 tsp kosher salt
2 Tbsp Mala Spice Mix
 (page 223)
2 tsp kosher salt
5 or 6 scallions, green
 parts only, thinly sliced
2 Tbsp vegetable oil
Soy sauce for serving
Sichuan Chili Crisp
 (page 220) or Chili
 Crisp Vinaigrette
 (page 226) for serving

1   Combine the flour with the hot water in a bowl and knead for about 5 minutes until a ball forms. The dough should be smooth to the touch, not sticky but not dry either. Add more flour or water, if needed, to achieve the right consistency. Cover the bowl with plastic wrap and let the dough rest for at least 30 minutes.

2   Lightly flour a flat surface and place the dough on it. Using a rolling pin, roll out the dough into a long rectangular shape about ½-inch / 1.3cm thick.

3   Using the back of a spoon or a pastry brush, spread the lard over the sheet of dough and sprinkle it evenly with the salt, spice mix, and scallions. Using your hands and starting at the end of the sheet closest to you, roll up the dough from one side to the other until it forms a log.

4   Using a knife or a bench scraper, cut the log into four roughly equal pieces. Use a rolling pin or the palm of your hand to flatten the log into a pancake about ¾ inch / 2cm thick. You can roll it thinner if you would like your pancakes to have a crispier texture or leave it thicker for a chewier mouthfeel.

5   In a large nonstick pan over medium heat, warm the vegetable oil. Fry the pancakes for 7 to 8 minutes, turning them over a few times until they are golden on both sides and cooked through.

6   Slice and serve hot with a dip of the chili crisp or chili vinaigrette.

SALIVA CHICKEN

Koshuiji, or saliva chicken, is also known by its more appetizing name: mouthwatering chicken. A taste of this dish easily reveals why: once you've tried it, it's difficult to look at poached chicken the same way ever again. The tender and juicy poached chicken thighs are draped in a balanced savory and sweet concoction of soy sauce and bright chili oil. The traditional versions use bone-in chicken, but I find boneless works just as well and is easier to maneuver. The key to this dish is the Zhong sauce, a sweet, savory soy sauce and chili oil mixture you can make ahead of time that adds depth and dimension to numerous dishes throughout this book. _Makes 4 servings_

1 lb / 450g boneless, skin-on chicken thighs
1 Tbsp Shaoxing wine
1 or 2 (⅛ inch / 0.3cm) slices ginger
1 or 2 scallions, white parts only

SAUCE
5 Tbsp / 75ml Zhong Sauce (page 224)
¼ cup / 60ml chicken stock
1 Tbsp black vinegar
1 Tbsp soy sauce
1 Tbsp minced garlic
1 tsp minced ginger
¼ tsp Ground Roasted Sichuan Pepper (page 218)

GARNISHES
Sesame seeds
Sliced scallion greens
Chopped cilantro leaves
Chili Oil (page 219)

1 In a medium pot over high heat, bring about 4 inches of water to a boil. Add the chicken, wine, ginger, and scallion to the pot and lower the heat to medium. Simmer for about 20 minutes, until the chicken is cooked through but still tender.

2 Meanwhile, to make the sauce: Combine the Zhong sauce, stock, vinegar, soy sauce, garlic, ginger, and roasted Sichuan pepper in a small bowl and use a spoon to mix thoroughly.

3 Prepare an ice bath.

4 Remove the chicken from the pot and submerge it in the prepared ice bath to cool down, about 15 minutes. Remove the chicken from the ice bath and, using a cleaver, cut it into about ¼-inch / 6mm chunks.

5 Arrange the chicken on a serving dish and pour the sauce over the chicken. Garnish with the sesame seeds, sliced scallions, cilantro, and chili oil to taste.

NOT TRADITIONAL
But Personal

Allow me to reintroduce myself. My name is Jing, but it hasn't always been.

I spent the last three decades of my life hiding behind "Jenny," a Western moniker I chose at age five to make life easier as a kid growing up in Europe. 婧 Jing, given to me by my late grandfather, means virtuous, feminine. 玄 Xuan, my middle name given to me by my nuclear-physicist father, means profound, abstract, and is a homonym for his field of study—string theory. Imagine burying all that, just to feel like you belong.

It's no wonder my search for identity and heritage later in life brought me back to China. I spent more than ten years there finding meaning and my place in the intersection of food with culture, tradition, and modernity. I delved deeply into Chinese food culture and its regional cuisines, so varied and diverse it felt more like a continent than a country. I was stunned by the depth of this five-thousand-year-old heritage that no one outside of China seemed to know about, and what started as a personal quest to reconnect with my roots soon became a passion project to shine light on this cuisine and culture.

The idea of tradition and "authenticity" never really sat right with me. It felt terminal, and the description didn't allow for the evolution of a culture or its people. When a culture doesn't evolve, it dies, and I wanted to help push it forward. I started to develop my own deeply personal expressions of these flavors. Like me, they were rooted in tradition but were also an evolution. I was finally starting to find my voice, with food as my medium.

This journey came to a head when I started the very first iteration of Fly By Jing, an underground pop-up dining concept. I named it as an ode to Chengdu's famous "fly restaurants," hole-in-the-wall eateries so good they attracted people like flies, and as a nod to my birth name, which I was just starting to reconnect with but still felt a bit uncomfortable responding to. I was beginning to peel back the layers, but there was still more work to do.

Fly By Jing, in its current form as a spice and condiment company, was born out of a suitcase. Whenever I took to the road to host a dinner somewhere in the world, my bags were packed full of high-quality ingredients that I couldn't get anywhere but China. I understood why–there was little demand from the West, stemming not only from a lack of awareness but also from hundreds of years of bias against the cuisine and its people. Manufacturers had no reason to export high-quality products when they were repeatedly told the market wouldn't pay more than bargain-basement prices for them.

But whether I was in New York, Tokyo, or Sydney, people instantly connected to these flavors. Seeing people from all walks of life connect with these flavors, which were so deeply personal to me, planted a seed. I thought to myself, how can I create more spaces of belonging like the one I was carving out here?

In 2018, I traveled to California to attend Expo West, the largest natural food show in the United States. Fly By Jing was still in its infancy stages, and I spent days wandering through thousands of stalls looking for other Asian food brands. I could barely find any, and not surprisingly, I found even less diversity within the buyers and retailers walking the halls. It dawned on me that not only were there entire groups of people being left out of healthy eating but that the size of this missed opportunity was massive, since this was clearly not representative of what America looked like or how it eats.

When I went back to Shanghai, I knew it was time to upgrade my suitcases packed with ingredients to something bigger. I decided to launch my business in the United States, with the spices and condiments I was creating in my kitchen so I could make these flavors accessible to everyone. I knew it was an uphill battle against centuries of false narratives about Chinese cuisine, but it was worth it if we could take back this narrative, help redefine it, and show people just how good high-quality Chinese food could be.

I launched my first product, Sichuan Chili Crisp, on Kickstarter that summer. Sichuan Chili Crisp is an all-natural chili sauce that I developed as a foundation for a lot of my dishes. It became the highest-funded craft food project on the platform. It was clear that people were ready for a new narrative about Chinese food, one that did not conform to preconceived notions of value, taste, and tradition.

I highlighted the ingredients that I had spent years sourcing in the mountains and countryside of China, starting from my restaurant days. Many of these had never been exported before, like Qingxi's elusive tribute pepper, a variety of Sichuan pepper so intoxicating and rare it was given exclusively as a tribute to the emperor, or the prized amber-hued caiziyou, cold-pressed semi-winter rapeseed oil that's been used in Sichuan cooking

for thousands of years for its health benefits and intensely nutty flavor.

I knew my products wouldn't taste like anything else on the market, because they weren't made like anything else.

I was finally getting closer to finding what I had been looking for when I first moved to China ten years before, a voice that was undeniably my own.

After launching Fly By Jing online in February of 2019, we grew from our initial Kickstarter base as word of mouth spread about our products and the media started paying attention to this versatile new condiment called chili crisp.

Despite our early traction, many of the investors I met with dismissed it as a fluke. For a long time, it felt like one step forward and two steps back. I was accepted at a prestigious tech accelerator, where business leaders told me to tone down my mission of rewriting false stereotypes and bringing diversity to natural foods and instead to just focus on the delicious attributes of the sauce, because "consumers aren't interested in the mission behind the business." White investors told me they had a hard time believing Chinese food faced any bias at all, because "that wasn't their experience."

These were the uphill battles I knew I would face in building this business, but it still stung to hear it. I was a kid again, on the first day of school in Germany, indignant to the gaze of my classmates, who I recognized even at my young age, saw me as "other." I had the simultaneous feeling of wanting to be seen and to disappear altogether.

I decided to bootstrap the business, learning the ins and outs of running a direct-to-consumer company along the way from books, podcasts, and the wisdom of other founders. The company grew slowly and steadily, until everything changed with the pandemic.

When Covid first hit the United States, things were scary and uncertain.

Increased tensions arose from xenophobia, trade relations soured, and overtly racist comments started popping up on our social media pages. "We don't need anything else from China right now." "What's this made of, bats?" Production ground to a halt in China. I braced myself for dark times ahead.

But surprisingly, when quarantines were initiated, things quickly started to change. Forced to cook at home, many reached for our products, since they made it easy to add complex flavor to the foods they were already eating. We were flooded with emails from customers telling us how much comfort our products had given them in difficult times.

I'll never forget that day in April 2020, when Sam Sifton, a food editor at the *New York Times,* published a story about us. Nothing could have prepared me for the impact. In one week, we sold more product than we had in the entire previous year. We became an overnight success, one that had been several years in the making.

But the elated highs of the moment quickly dropped down to the lowest of lows as the reality of the pandemic's impact on global supply chains hit me. We sold out of many months of inventory in a few days, as I scrambled to restart production in China, where the factories were just starting to come back to life after several months of strict lockdowns.

I wish I could say all was smooth sailing from there, but I could fill a saga with the comedy of errors that ensued over the next four months, as I battled global logistics delays and "random" customs inspections. To speed things up, I found a US-based co-packer to help bottle the sauces, but the machines instantly broke under the weight of our sauce, forcing us to bottle thirty thousand jars by hand.

And even though our tide of support rose, the crescendo of racially charged comments online kept taunting me in full force. This was the same reductive dismissal that I had been hearing for years, whether explicitly from potential investors or implicitly from the stubbornly whitewashed natural foods industry. It was a narrative that stripped Chinese food and its people of their value. And at the end of this long road, I was exhausted. I was done convincing people of my worth.

Fighting for acceptance was a feeling I was all too familiar with. As a child of immigrants who had had to prove themselves and their right to exist everywhere they went, I was naturally conditioned to achieve. My feelings of self-worth, internalized at a young age, were measured in accomplishment and output.

When I think back to the late nights laboring over my stove in Shanghai, those long, exasperating days at factories in rural Sichuan, or crying in the bathroom of an office building after yet another investor I met had dismissed me and my vision, I persevered the only way I knew how: by donning a hard shield, emblazoned for battle. I fought so hard for an illusion of me, that I no longer knew the person beneath the exterior.

A few weeks into the quarantine, something shifted. It dawned on me that I couldn't recall the last time I hadn't felt the need for my protective armor. Incredibly, I felt at peace in just being. I no longer felt like the battle-worn Jenny whom I had known for the last three decades of my life. She had carried me far, but it was time to peel back the layers. It turns out that what I had been seeking all this time was right there within me.

That was the day I came back to Jing.

In a world that was constantly demanding justification for my existence, by embracing my birth name, it finally felt like a small but radical form of self-love and acceptance.

Since the day I reclaimed my name, I have felt a deeper connection to my purpose and a clarity of my mission and voice. I have come to realize that my past drive to achieve was fueled by a state of fear and contraction, the need to prove myself to

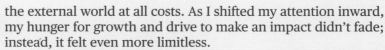

the external world at all costs. As I shifted my attention inward, my hunger for growth and drive to make an impact didn't fade; instead, it felt even more limitless.

I'm grateful to be living in a time when we're finally beginning to create space for all the diverse and multifaceted voices of our cultures to be celebrated and expressed, in our own way and on our own terms. The landscape of natural food in this country is changing, faster than I ever thought possible.

We've come a long way since those days when I stood over a wok in my tiny Shanghai kitchen. As I think about this evolution and all that we have yet to become, I'm proud to be at the helm of a brand that tells a deeply personal tale of seeking belonging and finding one's way home.

I hope that others will see a piece of themselves in this story of breaking free from tradition and writing new narratives and that something as simple as a name and a jar of chili sauce can be a radical reclamation of personal power.

Food has always been political—Chinese food has long been painted as a monolith and molded into narratives that fit neatly in our collective biases. But it's easy to be reductive when our exposure to others has been so limited. There is no room for complexity if everything is binary.

Like its people, Chinese flavors are complex, ever evolving, and diverse. We are more than a monolith. What started as my personal quest to reconnect with my roots has become a mission to celebrate the many layered stories of the diaspora, because real stories are personal, and they deserve to be told.

If I could travel back in time to little Jing, before she made the fateful decision to change her name, I would tell her that she is worthy, just as she is, and that there has always been a seat for her at the table.

Fly By Jing is the product of a personal journey of discovery and coming home to self. Like me, it was born in Chengdu but lives in America. It's rooted in tradition but made for the way we live today. It doesn't conform to anyone else's notions of value, taste, or tradition.

It's one person's recipes, one person's vision, and one person's story.

And with these flavors, I'm telling you mine.

76 Strange-Flavor Mixed Nuts
79 Mala Lotus Root Chips
80 Liangfen Jelly Noodles
83 Chili Oil Chaoshou
84 Zhong Dumplings
87 Wagyu Cheeseburger Pot Stickers
88 Sichuan Popcorn Chicken
91 Tingly Beef Guokui
92 Zhong Spam Musubi

STREET SNACKS

STRANGE-FLAVOR MIXED NUTS

A famous snack in Sichuan that I grew up eating is "strange-flavor" fava beans—crispy, crunchy fava beans fried and coated in a sugary, spicy, salty, and tingly coating. They are absolutely addictive and are usually served alongside afternoon tea in the park or as an equivalent to snacking nuts at the bar. Since it's hard to find fava beans as readily in the United States, I've substituted with an assortment of mixed nuts. These are a delicious treat and make for great hostess gifts. For a bit of a different flavor profile that's just as enticing, you can also substitute the chili and Sichuan pepper mixture used here with about a tablespoon of mala spice mix (page 223). *Makes 4 servings*

½ tsp kosher salt
½ Tbsp Ground Chili Powder (page 218)
½ tsp Ground Roasted Sichuan Pepper (page 218)
6 Tbsp water, or as needed
1 cup / 200g granulated sugar
½ lb / 225g assorted nuts (such as cashews, peanuts, almonds, and pecans)

1 In a small bowl, mix the salt, chili powder, and roasted Sichuan pepper together.

2 Set aside a baking pan.

3 In a large wok or pot over high heat, combine the water and sugar. Using a spatula, continuously stir the mixture as it begins to bubble and thicken for about 15 minutes, until it reaches 250°F / 120°C on a candy thermometer. Immediately remove the wok from the heat. Working quickly, since the candy liquid hardens rapidly, add the nuts and the spice mix to the wok, using a spatula to fold and coat them evenly in the sugar mixture; make sure to separate the nuts into small clusters.

4 Spread the nuts in a flat layer on the pan to cool for a few hours. They can be eaten after this cooling period but are best after resting for a day. They can be stored in an airtight container for up to 2 weeks at room temperature.

MALA LOTUS ROOT CHIPS

I like to think of these as the healthier version of potato chips. Sliced thinly and fried to a golden crisp, lotus root chips are gluten free, an excellent source of fiber, and are the perfect canvas for your seasonings of choice. I love how the versatility of mala spice mix shines here, but you can also simply season with sea salt or togarashi, a Japanese mixed chili powder.

Makes 4 servings

2 lotus roots
(approximately
1 lb / 450g)
1 Tbsp unseasoned
rice vinegar
Neutral oil for frying
3 Tbsp Mala Spice Mix
(page 223), or as
needed

1 To prepare the lotus roots: Wash the roots thoroughly. Using a mandoline, slice them very thinly into uniform rounds.

2 In a medium bowl, add the root slices, rice vinegar, and enough water to cover. Soak the slices for about 10 minutes, then drain and let dry, patting them with paper towels if needed.

3 Line a plate with paper towels.

4 In a wok or other pan over high heat, add about 3 inches / 7.5cm oil and heat until it reaches 350°F / 175°C on an instant-read thermometer. Working in batches, drop in the lotus slices, making sure not to overcrowd the wok. Use a spatula or chopsticks to move the pieces around so they don't stick to each other and fry for about 5 minutes, until the slices are golden brown, crispy, but not burnt. Using a slotted spoon or mesh strainer, transfer the lotus chips to the prepared plate to soak up any excess oil. While still hot, season with the spice mix to taste.

5 Enjoy immediately or store in an airtight container at room temperature for up to 1 week.

LIANGFEN JELLY NOODLES

These noodles, also called shangxing liangfen, or heartbreak noodles, are said to be so spicy they can bring you to tears. Sichuan chefs are famous for their ability to make noodles out of seemingly any starch. They use anything and everything from rice, mung bean, sweet potato, and split peas that are ground up to form slippery jelly noodles with a cool and silken texture. One of my favorites is made from mung bean starch and makes for a deceptively simple and impressive snack or appetizer. You can make this dish ahead of time—the longer it sits in the sauce, the tastier it gets. *Makes 4 servings*

½ cup / 65g mung bean
    starch
3 cups / 720ml water

SAUCE
½ cup / 120ml Chili Crisp
    Vinaigrette (page 226)
2 garlic cloves, minced
1 tsp toasted sesame oil
1 Tbsp sliced bird's-eye
    chilies (optional)
1 tsp Chili Oil (page 219)
    or Tribute Pepper Oil
    (page 219); optional)

Sliced scallions, green
    and white parts,
    for garnish
Roasted peanuts
    for garnish

1   In a medium bowl, combine the starch with 1 cup / 240ml of the water and mix until the starch has dissolved and is completely free of clumps.

2   In a medium pot over high heat, bring the remaining 2 cups / 480ml water to a boil, then lower the heat to a simmer. Add the starch mixture slowly into the pot, whisking the whole time to ensure no clumps form. Let the mixture simmer for another few minutes, continuously stirring as the mixture becomes a thick, almost pastelike texture. Then, carefully pour the mixture into a 9 by 13-inch / 23 by 33cm glass baking dish. Let it cool at room temperature for a few hours, until it fully solidifies into a jelly.

3   Place a cutting board over the baking dish and flip the dish upside down onto the board. You may need to jiggle the dish to loosen it up a bit. Once the jelly is on the board, cut it into bite-size pieces. Typically, the jelly is served as thick, rectangular-shaped noodles about 3 inches / 7.5cm long with a uniform thickness of about ¼ inch / 6mm, but I've seen them thinner or thicker, depending on the texture preferred. Place the noodles in a serving bowl.

4   To make the sauce: In a small bowl, combine the chili vinaigrette, garlic, sesame oil, and chilies, mix well, and pour over the jelly noodles. (For a slightly less hot version, omit the chilies.)

5   Let the noodles soak in the sauce for a few hours before serving. The longer they sit in the sauce, the tastier they will be. You can also add chili oil for extra heat or some tribute oil for more tingle. Garnish the dish with a sprinkling of the scallions and peanuts.

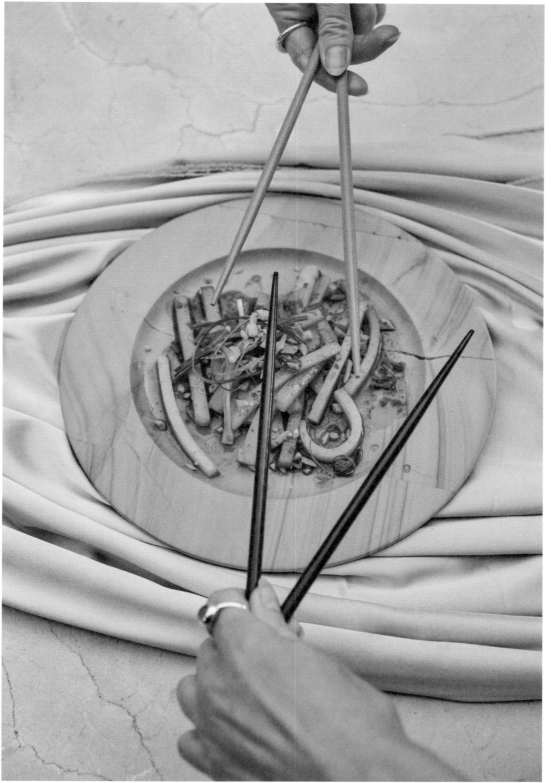

CHILI OIL CHAOSHOU

Chaoshou, the name in the Sichuan dialect for wontons, translates to "crossing hands," a reference to the way their square wrappers are folded into a triangle, with one point crossed over the other. In Sichuan, they are often served for breakfast or as an anytime snack in a hot broth or dry, mixed with chili oil, soy sauce, and aromatics. The thin wrappers hold small parcels of well-seasoned minced pork, and, when boiled, the chaoshou has a silky, slippery texture that's perfect for sopping up excess chili oil and sauce. My favorite is the classic Chengdu street-side version below of hongyou chaoshou, or chili oil wontons. *Makes 6 servings*

FILLING
1 (2-inch / 5cm) piece ginger
1 large scallion, white and green parts, chopped
¼ cup / 60ml water
½ lb / 225g ground pork (30% fat, 70% lean)
1 egg
1 tsp Shaoxing wine
1 tsp toasted sesame oil
½ tsp kosher salt
¼ tsp ground white pepper

12 oz / 340g wonton skins

SAUCE
2 Tbsp Sichuan Chili Crisp (page 220)
2 Tbsp Chili Oil (page 219)
3 Tbsp light soy sauce
¼ cup /60ml chicken stock, warmed
2 tsp kosher salt
½ tsp Ground Roasted Sichuan Pepper (page 218)
1 tsp Ground Chili Powder (page 218)
1 tsp roasted sesame seeds
1 or 2 thinly sliced scallions, green parts only

1 To make the filling: Smash the ginger with the flat side of a cleaver until it is crushed, then coarsely chop. In a small bowl, combine the ginger and scallion with the water and set aside to soak.

2 In a medium bowl, add the pork, egg, wine, sesame oil, salt, and pepper and mix vigorously to combine. Remove the ginger and scallion from the water and discard. Pour the soaking water gradually into the meat mixture, combining the water with the meat until it is fully incorporated and becomes a light and springy paste.

3 Line a baking tray with wax paper.

4 Take a wonton skin and smear about ½ Tbsp / 15g of the meat mixture into the center with a spoon. Using your finger, wet the perimeter with some water and then fold the wonton skin diagonally into a triangle. Press down to seal the sides. Place the triangle into your palm with a tip facing your wrist, slightly bend your middle finger toward you and crease the triangle in the middle. Dab a bit of water on one corner and bring the other corner on top to seal it. The wonton should now sit straight up when you place it on a flat surface. Work through your meat mixture and wonton skins until you run out of one or both, placing your wontons as they're done on the prepared tray. You can freeze any wontons you're not planning on eating straight away for up to 3 months. To freeze, place the wontons in a single layer on a tray in the freezer. Once frozen, store the wontons in a resealable bag to save on space.

5 To make the sauce: In a medium bowl, combine the chili crisp, chili oil, soy sauce, stock, salt, roasted Sichuan pepper, chili powder, sesame seeds, and scallions and mix. Divide the sauce among six bowls.

6 In a large pot over high heat, bring water to a boil. Working in batches of about ten, so as not to overcrowd the pot, cook the wontons. They should start to float up to the surface after 3 to 4 minutes. Wait another minute or so, then, using a slotted spoon, remove them from the pot. Place about six to eight wontons into each bowl and serve hot!

ZHONG DUMPLINGS

My identity is wrapped around Zhong dumplings, one of the most famous street snacks in Chengdu. I've been obsessed with them since childhood, and I still picture my first bite at a fly restaurant near my grandparents' house, the chili oil dribbling down my chin and my eyes wide as I tasted the indescribably delicious combination of juicy pork, sweet soy sauce, garlic, and sesame. I was instantly hooked, and years later, this was the core memory that brought me back to Chengdu to begin my journey of building Fly By Jing. Since I first started cooking in my supper club in Shanghai, I've been trying to perfect a version of this dish. I think I've come pretty close here. I've served these dumplings over the years at hundreds of events. They're always—always!—the first to disappear. _Makes 6 servings_

SAUCE
½ cup / 100g dark brown sugar, lightly packed
2 or 3 pieces star anise
2 dried shiitake mushrooms
1 piece cassia bark (1 to 2 inch / 2.5 to 5cm)
½ cup / 120ml light soy sauce
½ cup / 120ml Chili Oil (page 219)
1 Tbsp black vinegar
1 large garlic clove, minced

FILLING
1 lb / 450g ground pork (30% fat, 70% lean)
1 Tbsp plus 1 tsp cornstarch
1 Tbsp fish sauce
1 Tbsp toasted sesame oil
1 Tbsp Shaoxing wine
1 tsp soy sauce
1 tsp kosher salt
1 tsp ground white pepper
4 scallions, green parts only, thinly sliced
1 egg
1 (1-inch / 2.5cm) piece ginger, minced
½ cup / 120ml water

1 (14-oz / 395g) package dumpling wrappers

1 To make the sauce: In a small saucepan over low heat, infuse the brown sugar, star anise, mushrooms, and cassia bark in soy sauce for 30 minutes. Remove the pan from the heat and cool completely before stirring in the chili oil and vinegar. Store in an airtight container at room temperature for up to 1 month or in the fridge for up to 3 months. Remove the spices with a slotted spoon before using.

2 To make the filling: In a large bowl, combine the pork, 1 Tbsp of the cornstarch, the fish sauce, sesame oil, wine, soy sauce, salt, pepper, scallions, egg, ginger, and water and mix well. If you'd like to test the meat's seasoning, fry a little bit in a pan with some oil. It should taste delicious and umami-rich with no other seasoning.

3 To form the dumplings: Put some water in a small bowl. Dip a finger in the water and wet the perimeter of a dumpling wrapper. Place about 1 Tbsp of the filling in the middle of each wrapper and fold the wrapper in half. Crimp the edges of the dumpling with your fingers to seal and form into half-moon shapes. Transfer the dumpling to a tray or large platter and repeat with the remaining wrappers. You can make these ahead and freeze them for up to 3 months. To freeze, place the dumplings in a single layer on a tray in the freezer. Once frozen, store the dumplings in a resealable bag to save on space.

4 To cook the dumplings: In a large pot over high heat, bring some salted water to a boil. Once boiling, drop the dumplings in, about a dozen at a time so as not to crowd the pot, making sure to gently stir right away so nothing sticks to the bottom of the pot. The dumplings should start to float to the top after 3 to 4 minutes. Wait another 15 seconds, then, using a slotted spoon, remove them from the water.

5 When ready to serve, in a small bowl, stir the garlic with 3 Tbsp of the sauce. Drizzle the sauce over the freshly boiled dumplings and enjoy! Store any remaining sauce in an airtight container in the fridge for up to 2 weeks.

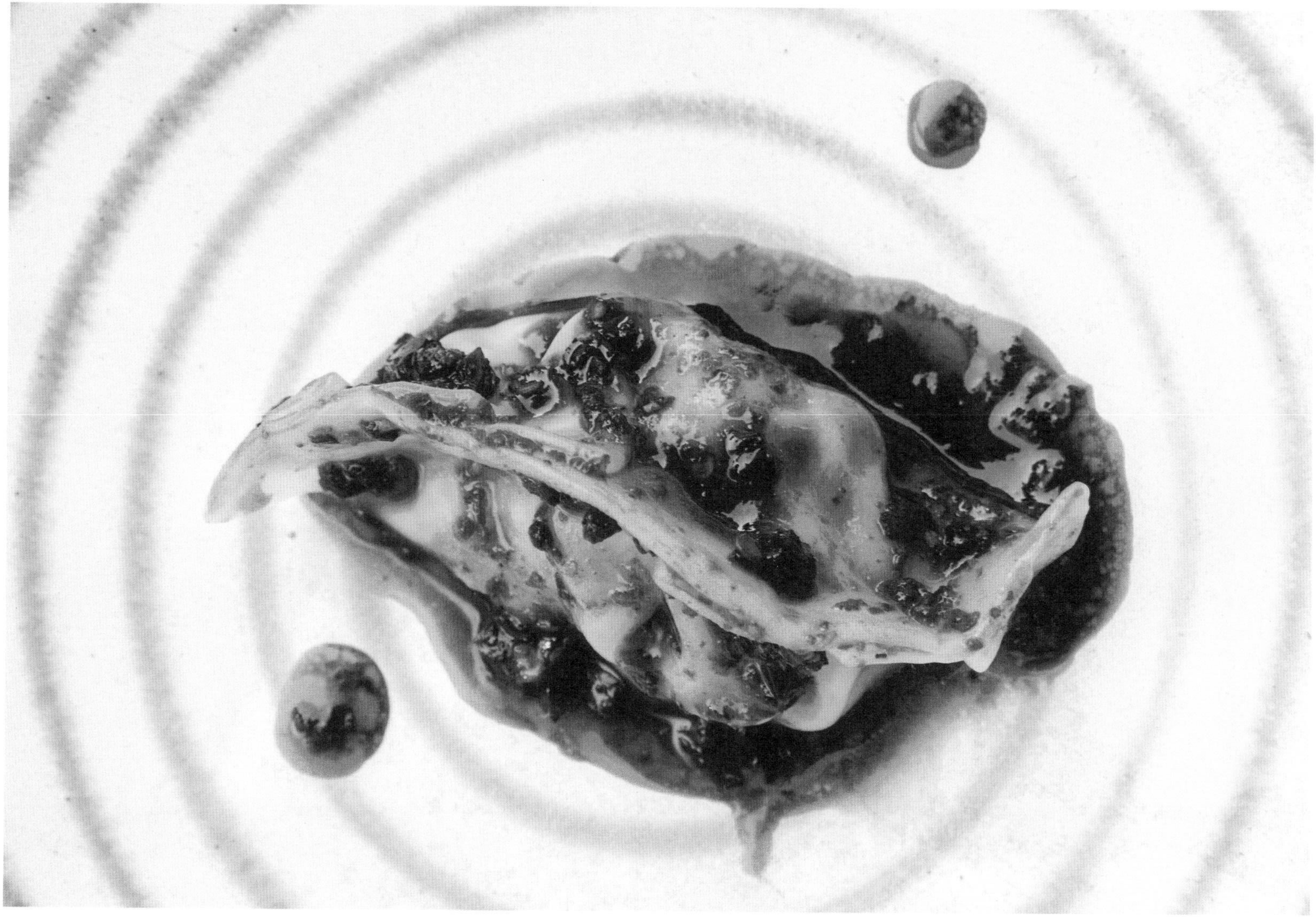

WAGYU CHEESEBURGER POT STICKERS

I've made countless variations of dumplings over the years, but none has gotten quite as emphatic a response as these, and it's no surprise why. Dumplings and cheeseburgers, two of some of the most perfect foods, meet to create magic, pulled together by a creamy and tangy chili crisp aioli. I like using ground wagyu because of its higher fat ratio that makes a juicier filling. *Makes 6 servings*

FILLING
6 oz / 170g bacon
1 lb / 450g ground
  wagyu
1 egg
1 cup / 120g shredded
  Cheddar cheese
¼ cup / 40g finely
  chopped dill pickles
¼ cup / 20g finely
  chopped shallots
2 Tbsp Dijon mustard
1 Tbsp fish sauce

1 (14-oz / 395g) package
  dumpling wrappers

2 to 3 Tbsp vegetable oil
  for frying

¼ cup / 60g Chili Crisp
  Aioli (page 226)

1 To make the filling: Preheat the oven to 400°F / 200°C. Line a baking tray with parchment paper.

2 Place the bacon strips on the prepared tray and cook for 15 to 20 minutes until they reach the desired crispiness. Let the bacon cool then chop into small pieces.

3 In a medium bowl, combine the wagyu, egg, bacon, cheese, pickles, shallots, mustard, and fish sauce and mix well.

4 To form the pot stickers: Put some water in a small bowl. Dip your finger in the water and wet the perimeter of a dumpling wrapper. Place about 1 Tbsp of the filling in the middle of each wrapper and fold the wrapper in half. Crimp the edges of the dumpling with your fingers to seal and form into half-moon shapes. Transfer the dumpling to a tray or large platter and repeat with the remaining wrappers. You can make these ahead and freeze them for up to 3 months. To freeze, place the dumplings in a single layer on a tray in the freezer. Once frozen, store the dumplings in a resealable bag to save on space.

5 To cook the pot stickers: In a large nonstick frying pan over medium heat, heat some oil. Working in two or three batches, so as not to crowd the pan, add the dumplings in a single layer and cook for a few minutes until the bottoms are golden brown. Then, add about ¼ cup / 60ml water (it should only cover a thin layer) to the pan and cover to steam the pot stickers for about 3 more minutes. When the water is almost fully evaporated, remove the lid and let the pot stickers cook for another minute or so. At this point, they will be fully cooked through and crispy on the bottom. Remove the pan from the heat and transfer the pot stickers to a serving plate. Repeat with the remaining pot stickers.

6 Serve the pot stickers with the aioli as a dipping sauce on the side.

SICHUAN POPCORN CHICKEN

This dish is an amalgamation of a couple of my favorite things, Taiwanese popcorn chicken and Sichuan's lazi chicken. The former is usually sweeter and crunchier because of its tapioca batter. It's served with fragrant basil leaves in a cone or a cup as a street-side snack. Sichuan's version is usually unbattered, fried with copious amounts of bright red dried chilies, and dusted in a potent mala seasoning blend. This dish is a party favorite and is always quick to disappear. _Makes 6 servings_

2 lb / 900g boneless, skinless chicken thighs, cut into 1-inch / 2.5cm pieces
3 Tbsp soy sauce
2 Tbsp minced garlic
2 tsp five-spice powder
2 tsp granulated sugar
2 tsp kosher salt
2 cups / 240g tapioca starch
2 eggs
Neutral oil for frying
1 Tbsp Mala Spice Mix (page 223)
1 cup / 15g Thai basil leaves, lightly packed

1   In a large bowl, combine the chicken with the soy sauce, garlic, five-spice powder, sugar, and salt. Set aside to marinate for at least 30 minutes or overnight in the refrigerator.

2   Have on hand two shallow bowls. In the first bowl, add the tapioca starch. In the second bowl, whisk the eggs. Working with one piece of chicken at a time, dip each piece in the beaten eggs, then in the tapioca starch.

3   Line a plate with paper towels.

4   Add 3 inches / 7.5cm oil in a wok over high heat and heat to about 350°F / 175°C on an instant-read thermometer. Working in batches, add the battered chicken pieces and fry until golden and crispy, 8 to 9 minutes. Transfer the chicken to the prepared plate and sprinkle evenly with the spice mix.

5   Quickly fry the basil leaves in the wok until crispy and translucent, about 30 seconds or so, and toss together with the fried chicken. Serve hot.

TINGLY BEEF GUOKUI

Guokui—a crispy, flaky, delicious flatbread snack, stuffed with savory or sweet fillings like beef or red beans—are some of the best bites of Chengdu's vast street food repertoire. The guokui are hand kneaded to order with lard, scallions, and minced pork or beef laced throughout the dough, then fried to a golden, flaky crisp and finished in a tandoor-like oven. Each bite is intensely savory, with a strong tingle of Sichuan pepper that lingers on your palate. *Makes 5 servings*

DOUGH
2 cups / 250g all-purpose flour, plus more for flouring the work surface
1 tsp kosher salt
⅔ cup / 160ml hot water

FILLING
½ lb / 225g ground fatty beef (wagyu works well)
2 Tbsp chopped scallions, white parts only
2 Tbsp Sichuan Chili Crisp (page 220)
1 Tbsp minced ginger
½ tsp kosher salt
2 tsp Ground Roasted Sichuan Pepper (page 218)
¼ tsp five-spice powder

3 Tbsp lard or ghee, melted
2 Tbsp sesame seeds
Neutral oil for frying

1 To make the dough: In a large bowl, combine the flour and salt and pour in the water, using a rubber spatula to mix and combine. When the dough cools down, work it with your hands and keep kneading it until it forms a ball. It should be slightly moist but not sticky; add flour or water to arrive at the ideal consistency. Transfer the ball to a lightly oiled bowl, cover with a damp kitchen towel or plastic wrap, and leave for at least 30 minutes.

2 To make the filling: In a medium bowl, combine the beef, scallions, chili crisp, ginger, salt, roasted Sichuan pepper, and five-spice powder and mix well. Place the bowl in the refrigerator until ready to use.

3 Transfer the dough ball to a lightly floured surface and, using your hands, roll it into a log. Using a cleaver or a bench scraper, separate the dough into five equal pieces. Shape each of the pieces into a ball, cover them with plastic wrap, and let rest for another 15 minutes.

4 To assemble your guokui: Remove one ball of dough and keep the remaining covered. On a floured surface and using a rolling pin, flatten the ball into a long dough strip about ¼ inch / 6mm thick and 4 inches / 10cm wide. Using a pastry brush, brush the lard onto the dough. Then take about 2 Tbsp of the filling and spread it evenly across the dough.

5 Starting from the bottom, slowly start to roll up the dough to form a log. Once your log is roughly 4 inches / 10cm wide, take one end and roll it toward the other end to form a wheel. Flatten the wheel with your palm. Repeat with the remaining dough. Sprinkle the sesame seeds over the middle of each guokui and use the rolling pin to flatten them out some more until each disk is about ½ inch / 1.3cm thick.

6 Preheat the oven to 425°F / 220°C. Line a large baking tray with parchment paper.

7 In a large nonstick frying pan over medium heat, pour enough oil to thinly coat the entire pan. Working in batches, place as many guokui as will fit in the pan and fry for a couple minutes on each side until golden brown. Transfer the guokui onto the prepared tray and bake in the oven for 5 to 6 minutes. Eat while hot!

ZHONG SPAM MUSUBI

This is an undeniably delicious snack, because well, Spam is delicious and Zhong sauce is good on everything. When the sweet, garlicky, chili soy flavors of Zhong and slices of Spam hit the pan, the resulting caramelization is out of this world. Musubis are really just an easy excuse to feel somewhat healthier about consuming ungodly amounts of Spam. Make and pack this for your next road trip, and you won't regret it. You will need a musubi press, which is easy to find online. *Makes 8 servings*

1 (12-oz / 340g) can Spam, cut into eight slices
¼ cup / 60ml Zhong Sauce (page 224)
3 Tbsp unseasoned rice vinegar
3 tsp granulated sugar
¾ tsp kosher salt
3 cups / 600g freshly cooked short grain rice
2 sheets nori, cut into eight strips
2 Tbsp furikake

1   Place the Spam slices in a resealable bag with the Zhong sauce and let them marinate for about 30 minutes.

2   In a small saucepan over medium-high heat, combine the vinegar, sugar, and salt and whisk until the salt and sugar are melted and the liquid comes to a simmer, 3 to 4 minutes. Remove the saucepan from the heat and drizzle the liquid onto the rice, folding it in gently until fully incorporated.

3   In a large nonstick pan over medium heat, cook the Spam slices in batches of two, with extra Zhong marinade spooned on top, until caramelized on both sides, 3 to 5 minutes total.

4   Situate the musubi mold in the center of a nori strip. Place ⅓ cup / 60g of the rice into the musubi mold and press down. Sprinkle the rice with the furikake and top with a slice of Spam. Remove the mold and wrap the nori around the musubi and wet the edges to seal. Make the rest of the masubi with the remaining rice and Spam.

5   You can consume musubis immediately or make them ahead, wrapping them in plastic wrap and storing at room temperature for up to a few hours. The rice doesn't refrigerate well, so try to consume the same day you make them.

ON CHINESE FOOD:
A Culinary Landscape Misunderstood

Chinese food is layered and divine, rich and diverse, simple and complex, historical and modern, and warm and ever evolving.

Chinese food is beloved by billions throughout the world. It's ordered, devoured, craved, and desired.

It is also misunderstood.

This last point has been the crux of my culinary journey. For the last decade, I've been working to shed light on the false narratives surrounding Chinese food. The culinary heritage that stems from more than five thousand years in China has been both ubiquitous in the West and exoticized beyond its true roots. People have expected Chinese food to be cheap, always cheap. They've also wanted it to be easy and quick and to fit into unfounded ideas of what they believe to be "authentic." In all this, the complexity of Chinese food and the richness of its origins have been diluted and overlooked. In short—Chinese food has been disrespected.

Chinese food expanded in America as a direct result of the 1882 Chinese Exclusion Act, the first US law that banned the immigration of a group of people solely based on race. But a loophole allowed merchants to operate restaurants—and thus, small family-owned restaurants started by Chinese immigrants budded everywhere. The owners kept prices low to attract business, but sadly, the exploitation of underpaid and overworked laborers was what made these cheap prices possible. The story of Chinese cuisine in America is one of resilience and survival in the face of xenophobia and racism that darkly continues to exist today.

Why is it so hard to find high-quality, natural Chinese food on grocery shelves? I began to witness this stark reality when I traveled to America for my pop-up dinners. I had to tote around my essential ingredients in a suitcase, simply because I could not find them anywhere outside of Sichuan. How could I when there was such little demand for these spices and concoctions from the West, where they were routinely dismissed? In 2018, when I first visited Expo West, the largest natural food trade show in the United States, I barely saw any Asian flavors, let alone Chinese ones. It was perplexing, considering there were more Chinese restaurants in America than every McDonald's, Burger King, KFC, Taco Bell, and Starbucks combined.

That same year, I launched my best-selling hot sauce, Sichuan Chili Crisp, on Kickstarter, where it shattered records as one of the highest-funded craft food projects on the platform. But despite our early success, we had no shortage of detractors. Many investors dismissed my early traction as a fluke and said: "Chinese food is niche; it will never cross over to the mainstream." And for every supporter, there were hundreds of others who swiftly discredited us online: "$15 for a jar of chili sauce?? Why is it so expensive?" "I could get this for $2 at my local Chinese supermarket!" "What a rip-off." "Any Chinese food that is 'high-end' isn't authentic and is a capitalist marketing attempt."

At first, I responded with lengthy explanations of the premium and rare ingredients I had spent years sourcing in China, the laborious technique involved in crafting the sauce, not to mention the obvious incongruity of comparing a product made by a bootstrapped start-up to those of megacorporations with their economies of scale. But then I got curious.

What was it that made people believe Chinese food was devoid of value? That the people dedicated to the craft and heritage of their cuisine didn't deserve to profit from their labor? It's worth noting that the same criticisms are rarely directed at white chefs creating "elevated" versions of dishes they claim to have "discovered" in their travels East.

There's a fascinating theory that attempts to explain this phenomenon. It's called the hierarchy of taste, a value judgment of different cuisines and cultures based on the socio-economic status of immigrants from those countries. In short, some cuisines, such as Japanese and French, are lauded and privileged, thus commanding higher prices, while others are looked down upon and not afforded the same reverence. It's the reason why steak frites is considered elevated cuisine while carne asada, a similarly high-quality cut of meat, is expected to be sold in street side trucks for change. And it's why ravioli and pasta command vastly different prices than dumplings and Lanzhou pulled noodles. In the hierarchy of taste, Chinese cuisine ranks as one of the lowest.

This dark truth became even more alarming to me when I began to see how people loved–absolutely loved–Chinese food around the globe. The flavors in my dishes, as well as those of other Chinese chefs, unlock a vibrance in people. People feel connected to the heat and experiences on their tongues. They widen their eyes over the uniqueness. It's often a surprise to them that Chinese food has all of this to offer.

The silver lining in all of this is that this hierarchy isn't rigid; it evolves just as living and breathing cultures do. It's worth noting that even though a plate of pasta can go for $40 today, the Italians and their foodways were similarly looked down upon when they first migrated to the United States a century ago. It's forever a privilege for me to be in a rising class of young chefs and food entrepreneurs of Chinese descent, working to honor and evolve the narrative of our cuisine and culture and help push it toward a more equitable future.

I love what Lucas Sin, my friend and Cantonese chef, once said about the need for cultural food education: "I'm of the opinion that the more people know about Chinese food, the better Italian food is going to get. The better French food is going to get. It's just that Chinese food is one of those cuisines that, unfortunately, especially in the United States and in the West, is oftentimes coupled with this idea that it's not of high quality, it's not technical, and that sort of thing."

The truth is, Chinese food is a million different things and versions, depending on whom you ask or what family is cooking it. Take chili oil for instance: There are thousands of different styles of chili oil in China, with every family safeguarding its own recipe. I've seen ingredients ranging from nuts and seeds to beef, mushrooms, and fermented fava beans. There cannot be a one-size-fits-all chili oil, just as there cannot be a one-size-fits-all view of Chinese food.

Like its people, Chinese flavors are ever evolving and diverse. What started as my quest to reconnect with flavor and my roots has grown into a mission to honor the stories of the Chinese diaspora.

Everyone has a story. Every dish has a truth. And they all deserve to be seen.

104 Mapo Tofu
107 Douban Fish
108 Pickled Mustard Green Fish
111 Sheet Pan Zhong-Glazed Salmon
112 Kungpao Shrimp
115 Lazi Chicken Wings
116 Spicy Three-Cup Chicken
119 Sheet Pan Mala-Spiced Roast Chicken
120 Ants Climbing Up a Tree
123 Red-Braised Pork Belly
124 Hongshao Carnitas Tacos
      124   Pickled Chili Pineapples
127 Kungpao Meatballs
128 Twice-Cooked Pork
131 Chili Char Siu Pork Jowls
133 Hot Pot is a Religion
139 Mala Xiang Guo

MAIN COURSES

MAPO TOFU

Mapo tofu is one of those "final meal" dishes I could eat every day. A bowl of this silky, garlicky goodness served over warm steamed rice is my definition of comfort food. It also happens to be one of the most famous dishes to come out of Sichuan. This dish is usually served topped with aromatic ground beef or pork, but it can just as easily be made vegan by substituting it with minced shiitake mushrooms or by omitting it all together. The umami of this dish comes from the deep funk of the doubanjiang, fermented fava bean paste.

The secret, of course, is in the sauce. You'll need a good doubanjiang and Sichuan chili crisp. I recommend using Fly By Jing's three-year-old doubanjiang and mixing it with an unaged regular doubanjiang. The aged version adds more complex flavor. I use a 1:1 ratio of aged and unaged. Instead of a vegetable or meat broth, I like to use bone broth for its rich, creamy texture and health benefits. I have also found that mapo tofu always tastes better when prepared in my clay pot donabe, and I refuse to make it in any other vessel now. Make this dish for people you deeply love! *Makes 4 servings*

14 oz / 400g regular or soft tofu, cut into ¾-inch / 2cm cubes
1 Tbsp neutral oil
¼ lb / 115g ground beef or pork
¼ cup / 60ml Chili Oil (page 219)
1 Tbsp minced garlic
1 Tbsp minced ginger
2 Tbsp doubanjiang
2 Tbsp Sichuan Chili Crisp (page 220)
¾ cup / 175ml bone broth or vegetable stock
2 tsp cornstarch
2 Tbsp cold water
2 scallions, green parts only, thinly sliced
¼ tsp Ground Roasted Sichuan Pepper (page 218)
White rice for serving

1 Gently place the tofu in a heatproof container, pour lightly salted boiling water over it so that it's fully submerged, and set it aside. This step will give the tofu a better flavor and texture and prevent it from breaking as easily.

2 In a wok or other pan over high heat, warm the oil, then add the meat, stir-frying until fully cooked, fragrant, and slightly crisp on the outside, 4 to 5 minutes. Transfer the meat to a small bowl and set aside.

3 In the same wok over medium heat, warm the chili oil, then add the garlic and ginger and fry for about 1 minute, until fragrant. Add the doubanjiang and chili crisp and fry for another minute, being careful not to burn the seasonings and aromatics. Add the broth and bring the mixture to a boil over high heat.

4 Drain the tofu and gently slide it into the wok. Using a rubber spatula, stir all the ingredients, taking care not to break the tofu. Add the meat back into the wok. Let the stock reduce for about 5 minutes so the tofu and meat soak up the flavors from the sauce.

5 Meanwhile, in a small bowl, make a cornstarch slurry by mixing the cornstarch and water. Add the slurry to the wok a little at a time, gently stirring it in. Keep adding until the sauce thickens to your desired consistency. Depending on the type of cornstarch you're using, the amount you need to use can vary.

6 Transfer the mapo tofu to a serving bowl and sprinkle it liberally with scallions and roasted Sichuan pepper. Serve immediately with rice.

DOUBAN FISH

This dish is incredibly warming and delicious and is a perfect main course for a lunar New Year feast or for any kind of special occasion that impresses, but one that is not terribly difficult to achieve. The quality of doubanjiang you use is important here, since it's the main event and gives the fish and the tofu its deeply layered umami flavor. I like to use the three-year-old fermented doubanjiang we sell at Fly By Jing, but if you can find regular unaged Pixian doubanjiang, it will do the job as well. The tofu adds visual and textural interest but can be omitted if you want to skip a step. *Makes 4 servings*

1 (1- to 2-lb / 450 to 900g) whole fish (such as sea bass or flounder), scaled and cleaned
1 tsp kosher salt
2 Tbsp Shaoxing wine
14 oz / 400g semi-soft tofu
3 Tbsp neutral oil

SAUCE
2 Tbsp neutral oil
¼ cup / 60ml doubanjiang
2 Tbsp Sichuan Chili Crisp (page 220)
2 Tbsp finely minced ginger
1 Tbsp finely minced garlic
3 scallions, white parts only, thinly sliced
2 cups / 480ml vegetable stock or bone broth
1 tsp granulated sugar
2 tsp light soy sauce
½ tsp black vinegar
1 tsp cornstarch
1 Tbsp water
1 to 2 Tbsp chopped cilantro leaves for garnish

1 Make a few shallow diagonal cuts on each side of the fish, then place it in a shallow dish. Rub the fish with salt, pour in the wine, and let the fish marinate for 20 minutes.

2 Carefully cut the tofu block in half and then into slices about ⅙ inches / 0.5cm thick. You can do so without taking the tofu out of the box it came in. Boil some water and pour over the tofu, submerging it in the container. Set aside.

3 Remove the fish from the marinade and pat it dry with paper towels.

4 Add the oil in a wok over high heat and heat until smoking. Add the fish and quickly fry on each side for 2 to 3 minutes, until the skin crisps up. Remove the fish from the wok and set it aside. Discard the oil.

5 To make the sauce: Heat the fresh oil in the wok over medium heat until sizzling. Add the doubanjiang and chili crisp and fry for 1 to 2 minutes, until fragrant and the oil is red. Add the ginger, garlic, and scallions, frying until fragrant. Pour in the stock, add the sugar, soy sauce, and black vinegar and bring the mixture to a boil.

6 Slide the fish carefully back into the wok and gently spoon the sauce over it. Turn down the heat to a simmer, cover the wok, and cook for 10 minutes, flipping the fish over halfway through.

7 Mix cornstarch with water and stir into the sauce until it thickens, about a minute.

8 Transfer the fish to a serving dish, drain the tofu and gently drape the pieces over the fish like a blanket, and serve immediately. Garnish with cilantro.

PICKLED MUSTARD GREEN FISH

If you've eaten at a Sichuan restaurant, you've most likely had shuizhuyu, a fiery pot of sizzling hot soup containing slices of tender fish fillets and what look like a thousand pieces of dried chilies and Sichuan pepper floating around in it. As delicious as shuizhuyu is, in my book, I think its lesser-known cousin suancaiyu, or pickled mustard green fish, is often the real star because of its addictive hit of acidity. The rich broth is spiked with the savory depth of lacto-fermented mustard greens that greatly complement the fish. The addition of bean sprouts and vermicelli that soak up all the flavor of the soup makes this a complete meal. You can find pickled mustard greens in brine, at your local Asian store. _Makes 4 servings_

1 lb / 450g white fish fillets (such as tilapia or flounder)
1 tsp kosher salt
1 egg white
1½ tsp ground white pepper
1 Tbsp cornstarch
4 oz / 115g dried vermicelli
4 Tbsp neutral oil
3 or 4 scallions, white and green parts only, chopped
4 or 5 (1 inch / 2.5cm) slices ginger
5 garlic cloves, sliced
4 erjingtiao chilies, chopped
2 Tbsp whole Sichuan pepper
2 Tbsp doubanjiang
1 cup / 250g pickled mustard greens, chopped into large pieces
4 cups / 950ml chicken stock or bone broth
½ tsp fish sauce
1 cup / 200g bean sprouts
1 bunch chopped cilantro leaves for garnish
White rice for serving

1 To prepare the fish: Using a cleaver, cut the fish fillets on the diagonal into ¼-inch / 6mm slices. Place the slices in a medium bowl and add the salt, egg white, 1 tsp of the white pepper, and the cornstarch. Using a rubber spatula, mix gently until the fish is evenly coated. Let it marinate for about 20 minutes.

2 To prepare the vermicelli: In a medium glass bowl, soak the vermicelli in hot water for about 10 minutes, until softened. Drain and set aside.

3 To make the soup: In a large wok or other pot over medium-high heat, warm 2 Tbsp of the oil, then add the scallions, ginger, garlic, half of the chopped chilies, 1 Tbsp of the Sichuan pepper, and the doubanjiang. Using a spatula, stir-fry for about a minute, until the aromatics are fragrant. Add the mustard greens and stir-fry for another minute. Add the stock, then increase the heat to high and bring the soup to a boil. Season with the fish sauce and the remaining ½ tsp of white pepper. Add the bean sprouts and cook for 1 minute.

4 Lower the heat to medium low and, using a slotted spoon, transfer all the solids into a large serving bowl or donabe. Add the softened vermicelli to this bowl as well.

5 Increase the heat to high and, using a slotted spoon, gently lower the fish slices into the broth. Stir the fish gently as the broth comes back to a boil. The fish will cook quickly, so keep an eye on the pot—as soon as the fish turns from translucent to white, 3 to 5 minutes, pour the soup and fish into the serving bowl with the vermicelli and the rest of the solids.

6 Sprinkle the remaining 1 Tbsp Sichuan pepper and the remaining half of the chopped chilies on top of the fish.

7 In a small pan over high heat, add the remaining 2 Tbsp neutral oil and heat until hot but not smoking, 1 to 2 minutes. As soon as the oil is ready, pour it on top of the fish and broth and listen for the sizzle. You can do this at table side for maximum dramatic effect. Garnish with the cilantro and serve immediately with white rice.

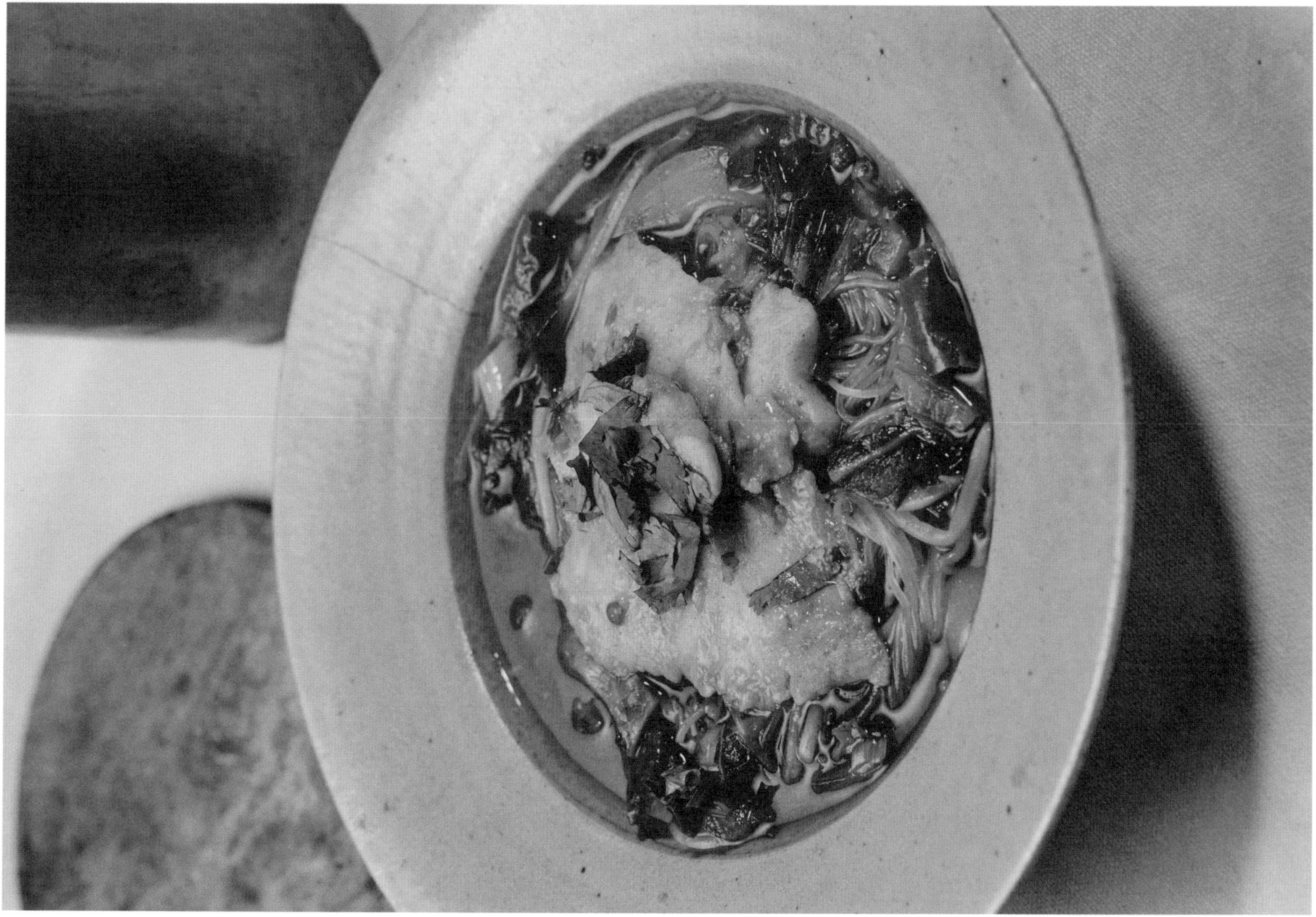

SHEET PAN ZHONG-GLAZED SALMON

If you're like me, you're often reaching for one-pan recipes that save on time but don't sacrifice on flavor. I love salmon for meal prep because it's one of the few types of fish that keeps well even when prepared two or three days ahead of time. Zhong sauce is a great marinade on most proteins, but I particularly love it on salmon. The brown sugar and soy sauce that form the sauce's foundation make for a rich, sweet, spicy, and savory glaze that caramelizes beautifully on the fish. This dish couldn't be simpler to make. Serve with brussels sprouts as below or with any kind of simple braised greens. _Makes 4 servings_

¼ cup / 60ml Zhong Sauce (page 224)
1 Tbsp honey
¼ cup / 60ml lemon juice
2 Tbsp minced garlic
1 tsp kosher salt
1 lb / 450g brussels sprouts, halved
4 (8-oz / 225g) salmon fillets
White rice for serving (optional)

1 Preheat the oven to 425°F / 220°C. Line a large sheet pan with parchment paper.

2 In a small bowl, combine the Zhong sauce, honey, lemon juice, garlic, and salt and mix well.

3 In a medium bowl, toss the brussels sprouts with 2 Tbsp of the marinade, then transfer them to the prepared sheet pan and bake for about 25 minutes.

4 Meanwhile, place the salmon fillets in a large resealable bag and pour in the remainder of the marinade. Seal the bag and place it in the refrigerator while the brussels sprouts cook.

5 After about 25 minutes, remove the tray from the oven and push the brussels sprouts to one side. Add the four salmon fillets to the tray and return the tray to the oven. Cook for another 15 minutes, until the salmon is fully cooked through and the brussels sprouts are crispy on the outside and tender on the inside.

6 Remove the tray from the oven and serve with white rice or just enjoy the salmon and brussels sprouts by themselves!

KUNGPAO SHRIMP

Kungpao, yet another classic flavor profile in Sichuan cuisine, is characterized by a balance of spicy, savory, sour, and sweet tastes. The sauce is versatile and can be applied to many canvases, most famously on chicken. I've made everything from kungpao eel to venison to tofu, but the version I frequently make is shrimp, since it comes together quickly. Take caution when you fry the dried chilies. Depending on how hot your chilies are, the room and your lungs might fill with smoke, so try not to take any deep breaths and definitely turn on the exhaust fan and open the windows. _Makes 4 servings_

2 Tbsp neutral oil
5 or 6 pieces dried chilies, cut into 1-inch / 2.5cm segments
1 tsp whole Sichuan pepper
1 Tbsp minced ginger
1 Tbsp minced garlic
3 scallions, white parts only, cut into ½-inch / 1.3cm segments
2 celery stalks, cut into ½-inch / 1.3cm segments
1 lb / 450g shrimp, peeled, tails on
½ cup / 120ml Kungpao Sauce (page 225)
½ cup / 70g roasted cashews or peanuts
Microgreens or edible flowers for garnish (optional)
White rice for serving

1 In a wok or frying pan over high heat, add the oil and heat until smoking. Add the chilies and Sichuan pepper and fry quickly so they don't burn, 10 to 20 seconds. Add the ginger, garlic, and scallions and fry until fragrant. Add the celery and shrimp and flash-fry for about 3 minutes, until the shrimp start to turn pink.

2 Pour in the sauce, stirring to make sure it coats all the ingredients evenly for 1 minute. The sauce will thicken as soon as it hits the heat, so move quickly here. Stir in the cashews at the very end before transferring to a serving platter.

3 Garnish with the microgreens (if using) and serve immediately with rice.

LAZI CHICKEN WINGS

Lazi chicken is another iconic dish that you've probably had if you've ever been to a Sichuan restaurant. Chunks of golden fried chicken are tossed in a fiery wok amid a sea of scorching red chilies and Sichuan pepper. At restaurants, the dish is usually served with small chunks of bone-in chicken, but I like to serve mine as wings, which are a bit easier to find in the pile of chilies. There is a gratuitous amount of chilies and Sichuan pepper that accompany this dish, but worry not, they're not meant to be eaten—they're only there to impart depth of flavor and heat. Sichuan chefs will fry their own peanuts for this recipe, but I like to use Huang Fei Hong brand spicy peanuts as a shortcut. *Makes 6 servings*

Kosher salt, for salting
  the wings
2 lb / 900g chicken wings
4 cups plus 2 Tbsp /
  950ml neutral oil (such
  as peanut or soybean)
Mala Spice Mix
  (page 223) for dusting
½ cup / 50g dried
  erjingtiao chilies,
  cut into 1-inch /
  2.5cm segments
1 Tbsp whole Sichuan
  pepper
2 or 3 scallions, white
  parts only, cut into
  thin rounds
1 bunch chopped cilantro
  leaves for garnish

1 Salt the wings liberally. Line a plate with paper towels.

2 In a large wok, or other pot big enough to deep-fry, set over high heat, add 4 cups / 950ml of the oil and heat to 250°F / 120°C on an instant-read thermometer. Working in batches, add the wings to the wok and fry for 15 to 20 minutes, until cooked through and golden but not brown. Remove from the oil and drain on the paper towel–lined plate. Rest and refrigerate the fried wings overnight in a flat layer, uncovered. Reserve the oil to refry the wings when ready to serve.

3 When ready to serve, in the same large wok over high heat, add the reserved 4 cups of oil and heat to 400°F / 200°C on an instant-read thermometer. Return the wings to the wok and fry for 5 to 10 minutes, until the wings are a golden-brown color. Remove from the oil and drain on paper towels.

4 Transfer the wings to a cooling rack and dust them liberally with the spice mix.

5 In the same large wok over medium-high heat, add the remaining 2 Tbsp oil and heat until hot but not smoking. Add the chilies, Sichuan pepper, and scallions and stir-fry until fragrant, about 2 minutes. Be careful not to burn the spices. Return the wings to the wok and add more spice mix to taste. Serve immediately, topped with a big bunch of the cilantro.

SPICY THREE-CUP CHICKEN

One of the seminal dishes in Taiwan's culinary tradition, three-cup chicken is both simple to make and rich in flavor. Tender bites of chicken thighs are draped in a luxurious sauce of equal parts soy sauce, sesame oil, and Shaoxing wine and served with copious amounts of aromatic basil leaves in a clay pot. Because I like the heat and complexity that Sichuan chili crisp adds to pretty much everything, I layer in a couple tablespoons during the cooking process here; the flavor melds beautifully with the sweet and savory sauce base. _Makes 4 servings_

2 lb / 900g boneless chicken thighs, skin on, chopped into 1-inch / 2.5cm pieces
2 cups / 480ml water
1 Tbsp kosher salt
¼ cup / 60ml sesame oil
4 or 5 (⅛ inch / 0.3cm) slices ginger
5 or 6 garlic cloves
1 or 2 pieces dried chili pepper
¼ cup / 60ml Shaoxing wine
¼ cup / 60ml light soy sauce
2 tsp dark soy sauce
2 Tbsp Sichuan Chili Crisp (page 220)
2 Tbsp granulated sugar
1 bunch Thai basil leaves
White rice for serving

1 Place the chicken in a large resealable bag. Combine the water and the salt to make a brine and pour it into the bag with the chicken. This will ensure a more tender texture of the chicken. Let the chicken sit for 30 minutes to 1 hour until you're ready to cook. Drain and set the chicken aside in a bowl.

2 In a large wok or clay pot set over medium-low heat, add the oil and bring to a sizzle. Add the ginger, garlic, and chili pepper, letting the aromatics infuse the oil for about 5 minutes. Increase the heat to medium high and add the chicken, searing until golden brown on all sides, 15 to 20 minutes. Add the wine, light and dark soy sauces, chili crisp, and sugar and stir to coat the chicken.

3 Bring the liquid to a boil, then turn down the heat to medium low, cover, and simmer for about 20 more minutes. Remove the lid, turn up the heat to high, and cook until the remainder of the sauce is reduced and it turns into a dark, shiny glaze, stirring often to prevent burning, 2 to 3 minutes.

4 Remove the wok from the heat and toss in the basil. Transfer the chicken and sauce onto a large serving dish or serve directly in the clay pot (if using). Serve hot with white rice.

SHEET PAN MALA-SPICED ROAST CHICKEN

This one-pan dish takes all of about ten minutes to prepare and is extremely rewarding. Make sure the chicken thighs are well seasoned with mala spice mix, which you can make ahead or purchase from Fly By Jing online. You can use any hearty vegetables, like carrots, potatoes, broccolini, or brussels sprouts, and the whole thing comes together in about 30 minutes in the oven. _Makes 4 servings_

1¼ cups / 300g carrots
  (4 or 5), cut into
  batons
1¼ cups / 300g fingerling
  potatoes (8 to 10),
  halved
1 small bundle
  (1¼ cups / 300g)
  broccolini
1 medium yellow onion,
  cut into wedges
5 or 6 garlic cloves,
  minced
4 or 5 sprigs rosemary
  or thyme
2 tsp kosher salt
2 Tbsp olive oil
2 lb / 900g bone-in,
  skin-on chicken thighs
1½ Tbsp Mala Spice Mix
  (page 223)

1 Preheat the oven to 425°F / 220°C. Line a sheet pan with parchment paper.

2 In a large bowl, toss the carrots, potatoes, broccolini, and onion with the garlic, rosemary, 1 tsp of the salt, and 1 Tbsp of the oil. Spread out the vegetables on the prepared tray. Then, place the thighs in the same bowl and toss with the remaining 1 Tbsp oil, the remaining 1 tsp salt, and the spice mix. Massage the seasoning into the chicken. Place the chicken on top of the vegetables on the tray.

3 Bake the chicken and vegetables for about 35 minutes, removing the tray from the oven once or twice to toss and turn the vegetables. Once the chicken reaches an internal temperature of 165°F / 75°C on an instant-read thermometer and the potatoes are tender, remove the tray from the oven and serve immediately. Store any leftovers in an airtight container in the fridge for up to 1 week.

ANTS CLIMBING UP A TREE

This was one of my favorite dishes as a kid, partly because of its fun name, but mainly because it's just so damn tasty. It's a famous Sichuan dish, featuring glass noodles in a savory, dark soy sauce and fragrant fried minced pork that clings to the noodles like "ants" when you lift them. The vermicelli is steeped in a complex stock of soy sauce, doubanjiang, and chili crisp, and all the flavor is soaked up into the strands during the cooking process. It comes together in a cinch and is the ultimate comfort food served on top of rice. _Makes 2 servings_

4 oz / 115g dried vermicelli
Neutral oil for frying
2 tsp minced ginger
2 tsp minced garlic
2 scallions, green and white parts only, chopped, plus more green parts for garnish
¼ lb / 115g ground pork (30% fat, 70% lean)
1 Tbsp doubanjiang
1 Tbsp light soy sauce
1 tsp dark soy sauce
1 Tbsp Sichuan Chili Crisp (page 220)
1 tsp granulated sugar
½ cup / 120ml chicken stock
White rice for serving

1 In a medium glass bowl, soak the vermicelli in hot water for about 10 minutes, until softened. Drain and set aside.

2 In a large nonstick pan with a lid over medium-high heat, heat about 1 Tbsp of oil. Add the ginger, garlic, and scallions and quickly stir-fry for about 30 seconds. Add the pork and fry for about 1 minute, stirring to break up into small chunks. Add the doubanjiang, light and dark soy sauces, chili crisp, and sugar, and continue to stir-fry for another minute, until the pork is evenly coated in the seasonings.

3 Add the vermicelli to the pan and pour in the stock. Stir the noodles around and fold the pork and aromatics into the noodles. Place the lid on the pan and cook for about 2 minutes, until the stock has mostly evaporated and the noodles are fully cooked through. Using tongs or a spatula, stir everything one more time to combine all the flavors. When you lift the noodles, every strand should be an even golden-brown color, and there should be bits of pork sticking to the strands. That's how you will know it's done.

4 Transfer everything to a plate and top with the scallions. Serve immediately with rice.

RED-BRAISED PORK BELLY

I fell in love with this dish when I lived in Shanghai. Hongshao, or red-braised pork, is the people's dish. Thick slabs of fatty pork belly are braised in soy sauce, rice wine, and sugar, until the meat is tender and the skin and fat have become gelatinous and melt in your mouth. The most famous version is from Shanghai, but versions of this dish have been developed all over the country, including in Hunan, where it is said it became Chairman Mao's favorite. Dark soy sauce is key to the color of this dish, and rock sugar gives it its beautiful glistening sheen. The addition of chili crisp gives it an extra dimension, and the resulting sauce is irresistible over steamed rice. _Makes 3 or 4 servings_

1 lb / 450g pork belly, cut into 1-inch / 2.5cm chunks
2 Tbsp neutral oil
4 scallions, green and white parts only, chopped into 1-inch / 2.5cm segments
¼ cup / 60ml Shaoxing wine
2 Tbsp dark soy sauce
1 Tbsp light soy sauce
1 piece (about 2 oz / 60g) rock sugar
1 cup / 240ml water
1 or 2 pieces star anise
1 piece cassia bark
½ tsp black vinegar
1 Tbsp Sichuan Chili Crisp (page 220)
White rice for serving

1 In a medium pot over high heat, bring some water to a boil and blanch the pork belly pieces for 2 to 3 minutes. In a colander, drain and rinse the pork with running water to remove all the scum and impurities from the meat. Set aside.

2 In a wok or donabe over medium-high heat, add the oil, scallions, and pork belly and fry for a couple of minutes, until the scallions become fragrant and the pork is seared and golden brown. Add the wine, dark and light soy sauces, rock sugar, water, star anise, and cassia bark. The liquid should cover most of the pork, but don't worry if it's not all submerged. Bring the mixture to a boil and lower the heat to the lowest setting, cover, and cook for about 1 hour.

3 At this point, the meat will be very tender, and your kitchen will smell incredible. Uncover the wok and turn up the heat to high. Once the liquid reaches a boil, it will start to reduce quickly, so pay close attention. Using a spatula, mix in the vinegar and chili crisp. After 1 to 2 minutes, the sauce will have reduced to a delicious thick consistency, coating the pieces of pork in a shiny, dark red elixir.

4 Transfer the pork and sauce to a serving bowl or serve directly in the wok. You'll want to serve some rice with this dish to soak up the ridiculously decadent sauce and the rich chunks of fatty meat. Store in an airtight container in the refrigerator for up to 1 week.

HONGSHAO CARNITAS TACOS

I made a trip to Oaxaca some years back and was amazed by the similarities between Mexican and Sichuan's foodways and cultures. And it's no surprise, when you consider that the chili peppers used in Sichuan cooking came from South America just a couple hundred years ago. There's a similar reverence for compounding flavors in the two cuisines. Heat is rarely used in isolation but rather layered and balanced with fragrance and flavor. Salsa macha is applied as liberally as chili crisp in Sichuan, and I especially loved the smoky, crunchy condiment on tacos. These tacos are my ode to carnitas tacos in Sichuan form, red-braised melt-in-your-mouth pork shoulder in a corn tortilla with melted Oaxacan cheese, pickled chili pineapples, and a chili crisp crema. A meeting of worlds that just makes sense! *Makes 4 servings*

1 recipe Red-Braised
  Pork Belly (page 123)

SAUCE
¼ cup / 60ml crema or
  sour cream
1 Tbsp Sichuan Chili
  Crisp (page 220)

8 corn tortillas or
  lettuce cups
⅓ cup / 50g shredded
  Oaxaca cheese
1 cup / 50g finely
  shredded red cabbage
¼ cup / 60g Pickled
  Chili Pineapples
  (recipe follows)
Chopped cilantro leaves
  for garnish (optional)

1 Ensure the braised pork belly is cool enough to handle. Using tongs or a fork, remove and discard the big pieces of dry spices and tear the pork shoulder into shreds.

2 To make the sauce: In a small bowl, mix the crema fresca with the chili crisp and set aside.

3 To assemble the tacos: When ready to serve, heat the tortillas in a pan on the stove over low to medium heat, two at a time. Sprinkle the cheese directly on the tortilla and melt. Divide the shredded cabbage and meat filling evenly across the eight tortillas. Top with the sauce and some pickled pineapples. Garnish with the cilantro, if using, and enjoy!

PICKLED CHILI PINEAPPLES

Makes 2 cups

½ lb / 225g pineapple chunks
1 or 2 red Thai chilies, thinly
  sliced
⅓ cup / 65g granulated sugar
1 cup / 240ml rice vinegar

Cut the pineapple chunks into smaller pieces about ⅜ inch / 1cm wide. Place them in a 1-qt / 950ml heatproof glass mason jar with the sliced red chilies.

In a small saucepan over very low heat, combine the sugar and vinegar and bring to a simmer, stirring to fully dissolve the sugar.

Pour the liquid over the pineapple, covering completely. Seal the jar and let it stand at room temperature to ferment for one day. The pineapple will be ready to eat the following day. You can store any leftovers in the refrigerator for up to a couple weeks.

KUNGPAO MEATBALLS

Another winning example of the versatility of Kungpao sauce, I make this dish often for potlucks and dinner parties. It comes together so easily, and most everyone loves meatballs! You can make the meatballs and mix the sauce ahead of time, combining them and letting them simmer until ready to serve. _Makes 4 servings_

MEATBALLS
1 lb / 450 g ground pork
   (30% fat, 70% lean)
½ cup / 70g grated onion
1 cup / 150g torn soft
   white bread
1 egg
2 garlic cloves, minced
¼ cup / 8g grated
   Parmesan cheese
¼ cup / 15g chopped
   flat-leaf parsley
¾ tsp kosher salt
¼ tsp black pepper

3 Tbsp neutral oil for
   frying, or as needed
¾ cup / 175ml Kungpao
   Sauce (page 225)

Sesame seeds for
   garnish
Chopped scallions,
   green parts only,
   for garnish

1   To make the meatballs: In a large bowl, add the pork, onion, bread, egg, garlic, cheese, parsley, salt, and pepper. Using your hands to really get in there, mix well to combine and ensure there is an even distribution.

2   To form the meatballs: Fill a small bowl with water—you'll use this to wet your hands as you form the meatballs. Using wet hands, take a golf ball–size mixture and form meatballs. You should have about twelve to fourteen meatballs.

3   In a large cast-iron skillet or nonstick frying pan over medium-high heat, heat about 2 Tbsp of the oil until sizzling. Add the meatballs and cook while turning until brown all over but not yet fully cooked, about 5 minutes. Transfer to a plate and set aside.

4   In the same large skillet over medium heat, heat the remaining 1 Tbsp neutral oil and then add the meatballs, followed by the Kungpao sauce. Turn down the heat to low and simmer for about 10 minutes, tossing the meatballs occasionally so they are evenly coated in the sauce.

5   Remove the skillet from the heat, place in serving vessel and garnish with the sesame seeds and scallions. Serve immediately. Store in an airtight container in the refrigerator for up to 1 week.

TWICE-COOKED PORK

Pork belly leaves an indelible mark because of its saltiness and fattiness. This recipe calls for patience and time. You'll need to prepare the pork by boiling and cooling it for a few hours beforehand. But once you've prepared your ingredients, the actual dish comes together quickly in a wok over high heat. Essential to this dish is doubanjiang, fermented black beans, and tianmianjiang, a type of sweet, fermented bean paste that is best known for its use in northern zhajiang noodles but occasionally finds its way into a savory dish like this one for a touch of funky sweetness. *Makes 4 servings*

1 lb / 450g pork belly (40% fat, 60% lean)
2 or 3 (1-inch / 2.5cm) slices ginger
2 or 3 scallions, white parts only, cut into 1 inch / 2.5cm segments
Neutral oil for frying
1 Tbsp doubanjiang
1 Tbsp Sichuan Chili Crisp (page 220)
1 Tbsp tianmianjiang
1 tsp light soy sauce
1 tsp granulated sugar or honey
1 Tbsp fermented black beans
1 medium leek, green part only, cut into strips about 2 inches / 5cm long
White rice for serving

1 In a large pot over high heat, add the pork belly and enough water to cover, then add the ginger and scallions and bring to a boil. Lower the heat to medium and simmer until cooked through, 15 to 20 minutes. Remove the pork from the pot and discard the rest.

2 Let the pork cool before moving it to the fridge to rest for at least 3 to 4 hours, until the meat is thoroughly cooled and firm; doing this will make the meat easier to slice. Once your pork belly is ready, use a sharp knife and from the skin side down, cut into slices as thin as you can. Set aside.

3 In a wok or other pan over high heat, warm 2 tbsp of oil until very smoking hot. Add the pork belly slices and fry them for 2 to 3 minutes, until they start to take on a little bit of color. Push the pork belly slices up to the side of the wok. Still on high heat, add the doubanjiang and chili crisp to the pan, and cook for 1 to 2 minutes, until fragrant. Add the tianmianjiang, soy sauce, sugar, and black beans and mix the pork belly back in, thoroughly cooking the meat, about 2 minutes. Add the leek and fry for 1 more minute, until it has softened but is still green in color.

4 Transfer to a plate and serve immediately with rice. Leftovers can be stored in an airtight container in the fridge for up to 1 week.

CHILI CHAR SIU PORK JOWLS

As you can tell by now, I'm a big fan of taking winning elements of different regional flavor profiles and applying them to my favorite canvases. Char siu, the iconic Cantonese roast pork that is delicious over rice, baked inside a fluffy steamed bun, or inside a glossy pastry bun features a sweet and shiny glaze made of five-spice powder, hoisin, and molasses. The char siu flavors happen to be a delicious marinade for almost any protein. I love using jowls because of how tender and juicy they are when prepared like char siu. There's a good amount of fat on this cut of meat that makes for incredible flavor, but you can trim down the fat to your liking. You can buy pork jowls precut in slabs at your local butcher. _Makes 4 to 6 servings_

MARINADE
¼ cup / 50g granulated
　sugar
2 Tbsp molasses
1 tsp five-spice powder
1 tsp kosher salt
4 garlic cloves, minced
¼ cup / 60ml hoisin
　sauce
3 Tbsp Sichuan Chili
　Crisp (page 220),
　or as needed
2 Tbsp Shaoxing wine
2 tsp toasted sesame oil

2 lb / 900g pork jowls

2 Tbsp maltose or honey
White rice for serving

1　To make the marinade: The day before cooking, in a large bowl, combine the sugar, molasses, five-spice powder, salt, garlic, hoisin sauce, chili crisp, wine, and sesame oil. Stir to mix well. Place the pork in a large resealable bag and pour ½ cup / 120ml of the marinade inside, massaging to coat the pieces of meat evenly. Squeeze the air out of the bag to seal and place it in the refrigerator overnight.

2　Microwave your container of maltose for 10 to 20 seconds to make it easier to work with. In a medium pan over medium heat, add the maltose and the remaining marinade, bringing the mixture to a simmer for about 5 minutes. Let the sauce cool, and then transfer to a covered container and place in the refrigerator.

3　To finish: When ready to cook the next day, preheat the oven to 450°F / 230°C. Line a large baking tray with aluminum foil and place a grilling rack on top.

4　Remove the pork and sauce from the refrigerator. Add a thin layer of water to the prepared tray; this will help keep the meat moist. Remove the pork from the marinade and discard the marinade. Place the pork on the grilling rack and bake in the oven for about 10 minutes.

5　Remove the tray from the oven. Using a pastry brush or spoon, generously baste the pork with the sauce on both sides. Flip and return the pork to the oven to cook on the other side for about 5 more minutes. Remove, baste again, flip once more, and return the pork to the oven to cook for another 5 minutes. Remove the pork and use the remainder of the sauce to baste it.

6　Turn on the broiler and return the pork to the oven. Broil for 2 to 3 minutes on each side. Remove the pork from the oven and let it rest on the grilling rack for about 10 minutes.

7　Slice the meat on the diagonal and serve with the rice. Serve with more chili crisp to taste.

More than just Sichuan's favorite dish (some locals eat it at least once a week!), hot pot is a way of life. It's said that the boiling cauldron of spicy soup wards off diseases, as the sweat you inevitably break into cools down your body from the inside and protects you from the dampness caused by Sichuan's humid climate. Consumed at restaurants or at home with family and friends, locals sit around a bubbling pot teeming with chili peppers, golden tallow, herbs, and spices and languidly cook a feast of ingredients washed down with baijiu, Chinese grain liquor.

Hot pot is served all over China, but what makes Sichuan hot pot special is its focus on the soup base over the dipping sauces. The soup base is a complex layering of flavors built upon a base of rich beef tallow, doubanjiang, chili oil, and up to a dozen spices and medicinal herbs thrown in for good measure. The result is a base of eye-popping flavor as a foundation for cooking an enormous variety of ingredients. Since so much flavor already imparts onto the ingredients as they cook, traditionalists will use only toasted sesame oil, minced garlic, and a sprinkle of MSG as a dipping sauce. But that doesn't stop new school hot pot restaurants (and those in other regions of China where the broth is milder) from featuring elaborate sauce stations, where everything from sesame paste, vinegar, chili sauces, and fermented tofu can be mixed to your heart's content.

Eating hot pot is a social event, and it's a marathon rather than a sprint. It's not uncommon for gatherings to graze languidly over the pot for hours, at which point the last remaining morsels in the pot can be terrifyingly spicy, sometimes to the point of hallucination. In the early twentieth century, some restaurateurs, hoping to keep customers coming back for more, heightened these physical sensations even further with the addition of opium in the broth. Though you can't find these spots anymore, creative restaurateurs have continued to find new and novel ways to get customers through their doors, with hot pot innovations like malatang and chuanchuanxiang, both variations of meat and vegetables skewered on bamboo sticks, cooked in spicy broth, and dipped in ground chili and sesame. The skewers can be served hot or, increasingly popular in summer months, cold as lengguo chuanchuan.

Hosting your own hot pot night at home could not be easier these days with so many ready-made soup bases on the market. I'm partial to Fly By Jing's version, of course; it's the first all-natural soup concentrate in the United States that's small-batch crafted in Chengdu. It has all the myriad spices and herbs that are impossible to get here and brings the flavors of Sichuan to your home in minutes. For all the flavor it packs, you'd be surprised to know it's vegan. But for those of you who want to try your hand at building a hot pot base from scratch, particularly the Chengdu version with beef tallow, this recipe is a good starting point.

HOT POT IS A RELIGION

HOT POT

SOUP BASE

4 or 5 pieces / 1.75 oz dried chili pepper

¼ cup / 20g whole Sichuan pepper

2 or 3 pieces star anise

1 or 2 pieces cassia bark

4 or 5 bay leaves

2 tsp ground cumin

2 tsp ground fennel

½ tsp ground cloves

2 black cardamom pods

1 cup / 240ml Sichuan rapeseed oil or soybean oil

1 cup / 250g beef tallow or Sichuan rapeseed oil

2 Tbsp minced ginger

2 Tbsp minced garlic

3 or 4 scallions, green and white parts only, chopped

½ cup / 135g doubanjiang

¼ cup / 60g Sichuan Chili Crisp (page 220)

½ cup / 120ml Shaoxing wine

1 piece (10g) rock sugar

1 Tbsp whole Sichuan pepper

10 pieces dried chili pepper

5 cups / 1.2L chicken stock, or as needed

HOT POT INGREDIENTS

Raw, thinly sliced meats (such as beef, pork, and lamb); available presliced at most Asian grocery stores

Raw seafood (such as shrimp, fish balls, squid, crab legs, and fish slices)

Heartier vegetables (such as potatoes, lotus root, daikon radishes, and pumpkin), sliced

Mushrooms (such as shiitake, enoki, oyster, and wood ear), cut into bite-sized pieces

Tofu products (regular, frozen, dried, or fried puffs), cut into bite-sized pieces

Seaweed in sheets, slices, or knots

Quail eggs, boiled and peeled

Leafy greens (such as sweet potato leaves, napa cabbage, spinach, and chrysanthemum greens)

Starches (such as sweet potato noodles, vermicelli, or konjac noodles)

DIPPING SAUCE BAR

Sichuan Chili Crisp (page 220)

Tribute Pepper Oil (page 219)

Light soy sauce

Black vinegar

Toasted sesame oil

Fermented tofu (furu)

Satay sauce

Sesame paste

Oyster sauce

Lots of chopped scallions

Lots of chopped cilantro leaves

Lots of minced garlic

MSG

1

To make the soup base: In a spice grinder or a food processor, coarsely grind the chili pepper, Sichuan pepper, star anise, cassia bark, bay leaves, cumin, fennel, cloves, and cardamom pods.

2

In a large wok or frying pan over medium heat, warm the rapeseed oil and tallow. Add the ginger, garlic, and scallions and cook until fragrant, 1 to 2 minutes. Add the doubanjiang and chili crisp and stir for another minute. Add the coarse spice blend, wine, rock sugar, Sichuan pepper, chili peppers, and cook, stirring [[AU: occasionally or constantly?]] for about 10 minutes. Pour the whole mixture into a heatproof container and set aside to cool. [[AU: How long to cool?]] (If using tallow, the mixture will congeal to a solid.)

3

To prepare the hot pot ingredients: Wash, chop, and place all the ingredients on serving plates and in bowls. Place a portable gas stove on your table and set a large, shallow pot in the center of the stove with the ingredients arranged around it.

4

Prepare to feast: Place the soup base into the soup pot over high heat, add the stock, and bring to a boil. Once boiling, turn down the heat to medium for a gentle rolling boil.

5

Invite your guests to mix their own dipping sauce of choice. The most basic dipping sauce in Sichuan is pure sesame oil with equal parts garlic, but I like to add soy sauce, vinegar, fermented tofu, chili crisp, scallions, and cilantro to mine as well.

6

Use long chopsticks or a slotted spoon to dunk ingredients into the pot to cook. Certain items, such as the quail eggs, lotus root, and tofu skin, can be cooked longer. Others, such as the leafy greens and thinly sliced meats, will cook very fast—just a light blanching will do.

7

As you feast, the liquid in the hot pot will evaporate over time, so be sure to add more stock or water to it. The broth will only get better over time, as you cook more and more ingredients in it!

MALA XIANG GUO

Mala xiang guo, also known as dry pot, is a popular variation of hot pot. The beauty of mala xiang guo is that you can use practically any ingredients. Because the vegetables and proteins all require different amounts of cooking time, there's a bit of precooking involved. Everything comes together at the end with the sauce, the key to which is the Sichuan hot pot soup base. It's often impossible to recreate outside of Sichuan, but if you'd like to try, I've included my own recipe on page 136. You can also use a store-bought soup base. Fly By Jing carries the first all-natural Sichuan hot pot base available in the United States, but you can find many other versions online or at your local Asian store. _Makes 4 servings_

VEGETABLES
¾ cup / 100g thinly sliced lotus root
¾ cup / 100g cauliflower florets
¾ cup / 100g quartered baby bok choy
½ cup / 50g wood ear mushrooms
¾ cup / 75g enoki mushrooms, torn into small pieces

SAUCE
2 Tbsp doubanjiang
¼ lb / 115g Sichuan Soup Base (page 136)
2 tsp granulated sugar

3 Tbsp neutral oil
½ lb / 225g shrimp, unpeeled, tails on
½ lb / 225g rib eye steak, thinly sliced

2 Tbsp minced ginger
2 Tbsp minced garlic
3 scallions, white and green parts, chopped into 1-inch / 2.5cm pieces
3 or 4 dried chili peppers
1 tsp whole Sichuan pepper
½ cup / 100g thinly sliced potato
12 quail eggs, boiled and peeled
½ cup / 75g fried tofu balls
½ cup / 70g dried yuba sheets, cut into bite-sized pieces
Chopped cilantro leaves
White rice for serving

1   To prepare the vegetables: In a large pot over high heat, bring some water to a boil and blanch the vegetables in batches, starting with the lotus root and cauliflower. Blanch for about 3 minutes, then, using a slotted spoon or a fine-mesh sieve, transfer them to a large bowl. Next, blanch the bok choy and wood ear and enoki mushrooms for about a minute, then, using a slotted spoon or a fine-mesh sieve, transfer them to the same bowl with the rest of the vegetables.

2   To make the sauce: In a medium bowl, mix together the doubanjiang, soup base, and sugar, then set aside.

3   To prepare the shrimp and steak: In a large wok over medium-high heat, heat 1 Tbsp of the oil and fry the shrimp for about 1 minute, just until it begins to turn pink, then transfer to a plate. Add an additional 1 Tbsp oil to the wok and this time, flash-fry the steak for about 30 seconds, just until it is cooked through. Transfer to the same plate as the shrimp.

4   To assemble the mala xiang guo: In the same wok over medium-high heat, warm the remaining 1 Tbsp oil and add the ginger, garlic, and scallions. Fry until fragrant, about 30 seconds, then add the chili peppers and Sichuan pepper, stir-frying for another 30 seconds. Add the sauce and let the fragrance from the doubanjiang and hot pot base release.

5   Add the blanched vegetables, potatoes, quail eggs, tofu balls, and yuba and increase the heat to high. Using a spatula, stir-fry and toss all the ingredients with the sauce. Finally, add the shrimp and steak and continue stirring to ensure everything is evenly coated with the sauce. Scatter the cilantro on top and transfer to a large serving bowl. Serve immediately with white rice. Store in airtight container in the refrigerator for up to 1 week.

144   Savory Soft Douhua

146   Hot and Sour Stir-Fried Potatoes

147   Fish-Fragrant Crispy Eggplant

149   Mapo Eggplant

150   Mala-Spiced Smashed Potatoes

153   Stir-Fried Chinese Greens

154   Chili Crisp Vinaigrette Cabbage

157   Chili Paneer

VEGETARĪAN

SAVORY SOFT DOUHUA

Douhua, or tofu flower, is a popular snack of tender tofu, served hot or cold and with sweet or savory toppings. Street vendors in Chengdu will often push around a cart with a giant pot of freshly steamed tofu and all the accoutrements in small containers. Layers of soft tofu are scooped out into individual serving bowls, and you get to take your pick of sweet, gingery syrup, or—more common in Sichuan—chili oil, chopped pickles, soy sauce, and cilantro. It's often served for breakfast, but I love it any time of day. If you're feeling ambitious and want to make your own tofu with fresh soy milk and a coagulant like gypsum, it will taste even better, but any store-bought soft tofu will do the trick. Here in California, I love Meiji tofu, a local family-run Japanese tofu maker, who make their tofu fresh daily in Gardena. _Makes 4 servings_

1 lb / 450g silken tofu

SAUCES AND TOPPINGS
4 tsp soy sauce
4 tsp toasted sesame oil
¼ cup / 60g Sichuan
   Chili Crisp (page 220)
1 Tbsp plus 1 tsp pickled
   mustard tuber
¼ cup / 40g fried
   peanuts
½ tsp Ground Roasted
   Sichuan Pepper
   (page 218)
2 scallions, green parts
   only, thinly sliced

1   To prepare the tofu: In a large pot over high heat, bring 2 inches / 5cm water to a boil, then lower the heat to medium and simmer. Place a steamer basket on top of the pot. Using a large spoon, divide the silken tofu into equal portions in four small bowls and place the bowls into the steamer. Cover and steam for 6 to 7 minutes.

2   To serve: Remove the bowls from the steamer and divide the sauces and toppings evenly on top of each bowl. Serve hot.

HOT AND SOUR STIR-FRIED POTATOES

I love the Chinese preparation of stir-fried shredded potato, and how it simultaneously achieves both crispy and tender textures. There are regional variations all over China, but the one I grew up loving was Sichuan's hot and sour version, characterized by a balance of heat from dried chili peppers and the pungent hit of black vinegar. You can use any kind of large potato here, just make sure to soak it in water ahead of time to remove extra starchiness. The dish comes together very quickly over high heat, so make sure you've done your prep and stir-fry briskly to avoid burning your spices or overcooking the potatoes. _Makes 4 servings_

1 large potato
2 Tbsp Chili Oil
   (page 219)
3 or 4 pieces dried
   erjingtiao chilies, cut
   into 1-inch / 2.5cm
   pieces
1 tsp whole tribute
   pepper
2 garlic cloves, minced
2 tsp kosher salt
1 tsp sugar
1½ Tbsp black vinegar
1 tsp fish sauce
2 tsp toasted sesame oil

1 To prepare the potato: The best way to get uniform pieces is to use a mandoline first to cut the potato lengthwise into ¼-inch / 6mm slices, then line up the slices into a stack and cut into thin strips with a cleaver.

2 Soak the potato strips in a large bowl of cold water for at least 30 minutes and up to overnight to get rid of the starch and to make it easier to stir-fry. Drain the potatoes and lay them out on kitchen towels to dry.

3 In a large pan or wok over medium heat, warm the chili oil. Throw in the chilies, pepper, and garlic and sauté quickly to release the aromatics into the oil, making sure not to burn the spices. Turn up the heat to high, add the potatoes and stir-fry for about 5 minutes, until the potatoes are still crisp but no longer taste raw. Season with the salt and sugar, add the vinegar and fish sauce, stirring to combine, then cover for another 2 to 3 minutes. Remove the pan from the heat, stir in the sesame oil, and transfer to a serving plate. Serve hot!

FISH-FRAGRANT CRISPY EGGPLANT

This dish is an adaptation of one of my favorite classic Sichuan dishes, yuxiang eggplant, and is a true expression of the deeply layered flavors of Sichuan cooking. In the traditional version, batons of fried eggplant are lathered in a sauce made of doubanjiang, pickled chilies, garlic, ginger, and scallions for a luxurious flavor kick that's warm and slightly sweet and acidic. The seasonings are similar to those used in fish dishes of the region despite having no fish in it. I love the OG, but in this version, I coat the eggplant in a mixture of starches for an unbelievably crispy texture that holds even after being tossed in the sauce, which I've adapted to be a thick, almost caramel-like consistency. This is a bit more involved, but trust me, you'll want to keep this dish on rotation. _Makes 4 servings_

BATTER
¼ cup / 35g rice flour
¼ cup / 30g tapioca
   starch
2½ tsp xanthan gum
1 tsp kosher salt
1 cup / 240ml water

SAUCE
6 Tbsp / 75g granulated
   sugar
2 Tbsp liquid glucose
½ cup / 120ml water
2 Tbsp doubanjiang
2 Tbsp Sichuan Chili
   Crisp (page 220)
2 Tbsp light soy sauce
1 Tbsp black vinegar
1 Tbsp minced garlic
1 Tbsp minced ginger
1 Tbsp sesame seeds
½ tsp Ground Roasted
   Sichuan pepper
   (page 218)

Neutral oil for frying
1 or 2 large eggplants,
   cut into batons
   2 inches / 5cm long

GARNISHES
2 long red chilies, thinly
   sliced
2 scallions, green parts
   only, thinly sliced
Microgreens

1   To make the batter: Mix the rice flour, tapioca starch, xanthan gum, and salt in a medium bowl. Add the water and whisk well until it starts to become a thick and goopy batter.

2   To make the sauce: In a medium saucepan over medium heat, combine the sugar, glucose, and water and whisk to dissolve the sugar. Bring the mixture to a boil and cook until it reaches 235°F / 112°C on an instant-read thermometer. Add the doubanjiang, chili crisp, soy sauce, vinegar, garlic, ginger, sesame seeds, and roasted Sichuan pepper. Lower the heat and simmer for about 25 minutes.

3   Line a baking tray with paper towels.

4   In a large wok or deep fryer set over high heat, add 3 inches / 7.5cm of oil and heat to 350°F / 175°C on an instant-read thermometer. Working in three or four batches, dip the eggplant batons in the batter and lower them carefully into the oil, taking care to not overcrowd the wok. Cook for 2 to 3 minutes, until the batter has hardened, then turn the eggplant over to cook the batons evenly for another 2 to 3 minutes, until the batter starts to turn a golden color. Using a slotted spoon, transfer the eggplant to the prepared tray.

5   In a large bowl, toss the eggplant with the sauce, stirring to make sure everything is evenly coated. If the sauce is no longer warm, it may harden slightly, so just reheat to get it to the right consistency again. Arrange the eggplant on a serving platter and top with the red chili slices, scallions, and microgreens. Serve hot.

VARIATION

To make the traditional version of this eggplant dish, make the batter and fry the eggplant batons as directed. Then place the batons in a large pan or wok over high heat and add ½ cup / 120ml Fish-Fragrant Sauce (page 228). Cook for 3 to 5 minutes, until the sauce has coated the eggplant evenly. Serve hot with rice and garnish with scallions if you wish.

MAPO EGGPLANT

There are very few things that mapo sauce doesn't enhance, and eggplant is no exception. This recipe swaps out the traditional tofu for eggplant, which has a similar soft texture but absorbs the rich flavors of the sauce even more. I include ground beef or pork in this recipe, but the doubanjiang adds so much umami that you won't miss anything without the meat. Serve hot over rice or as a topping over noodles. *Makes 4 servings*

1 Tbsp neutral oil
¼ lb / 115g ground beef or pork (optional)
¼ cup / 60ml Chili Oil (page 219)
1 Tbsp minced garlic
1 Tbsp minced ginger
2 Tbsp doubanjiang
2 Tbsp Sichuan Chili Crisp (page 220)
2 lb / 900g eggplant, cut into 1- to 2-inch / 2.5 to 5cm pieces
1 cup / 240ml bone broth or vegetable stock
2 tsp soy sauce
2 tsp granulated sugar
2 tsp cornstarch
2 Tbsp cold water
2 scallions, green parts only, thinly sliced
¼ tsp Ground Roasted Sichuan Pepper (page 218)
White rice or noodles for serving

1 If using the ground meat, in a wok over high heat, warm the neutral oil. Add the ground meat and stir-fry for 4 to 5 minutes, until fully cooked, fragrant, and slightly crisp on the outside. Transfer to a bowl and set aside.

2 In the same wok, bring the chili oil to medium heat. Add the garlic and ginger and stir-fry for about 1 minute, until fragrant. Add the doubanjiang and chili crisp and stir-fry for another minute, being careful not to burn the seasonings and aromatics. Then add the eggplant, broth, soy sauce, and sugar and bring the mixture to a boil. Lower the heat to medium low, cover, and simmer for 8 to 10 minutes, until the eggplant is cooked through. Add the ground meat back to the wok, if using.

3 Meanwhile, make a cornstarch slurry by mixing the cornstarch and cold water together. Add it to the wok a little at a time and gently stir it in. Keep adding the slurry until the sauce thickens. (Depending on the type of cornstarch you're using, the amount you need to use can vary.)

4 Transfer everything to a serving plate and garnish with the scallions and roasted Sichuan pepper. Serve immediately with white rice or noodles.

MALA-SPICED SMASHED POTATOES

This is my ultimate no-recipe recipe. I adore potatoes in any form, and smashed crispy potatoes find their way onto my dinner table at least weekly. If you're in a rush, you can use a cast-iron skillet instead of an oven; this will speed up the cooking time by about half. But if you want to set it and forget it while you're prepping the rest of your dinner, just let the oven do the work. The more edges and ridges you create while smashing the potatoes, the more delicious crunch and surface area to catch the mala spice mix seasoning. _Makes 4 servings_

1½ lb / 680g small
   potatoes
3½ Tbsp butter, melted
1 Tbsp kosher salt
2 to 3 Tbsp Mala Spice
   Mix (page 223)

1   In a large pot over high heat, bring about 5 inches / 13cm of salted water to a boil. Add the potatoes and cook until they are soft. Small ones should take 20 to 25 minutes, and larger ones might take 30 minutes.

2   Preheat the oven to 350°F / 175°C.

3   Drain the potatoes. Transfer to a baking sheet. Using a large fork or a potato masher, smash them while keeping them in one piece. Drizzle the butter over the potatoes, sprinkle with the salt and spice mix to taste.

4   Bake for about 40 minutes, until deep golden and crispy. Serve hot.

STIR-FRIED CHINESE GREENS

I've always found the diversity and range of Chinese greens to be vastly superior to Western greens, and it continues to surprise me how few of them are available outside of Asian markets, especially when the preparation for almost all of them is as simple as a stir-fry. Some of my favorites include morning glory (also known as water spinach), snow pea shoots, sweet potato leaves, and Malabar spinach. The Chinese even stir-fry iceberg lettuce, and trust me, it is delicious. The most basic cooking style is stir-frying, usually with ginger and garlic, done quickly over high heat in a wok, so that the vegetables are cooked through but remain bright green in color. You can also blanch and serve the greens with oyster sauce, which generally works better on vegetables with heartier stems such as bok choy and gai lan. Another way to consume these greens is in broth. I love dipping leafy greens into my hot pot or adding them to congees. Vegetables like chrysanthemum greens and red amaranth work especially well here. The recipe below is for a simple stir-fry. I love the umami that fish sauce adds, but you can omit it for a vegan version. *Makes 2 servings*

2 cups / 400g Chinese leafy greens (such as sweet potato leaves, pea shoots, and water spinach)
1 Tbsp neutral oil
1 or 2 pieces dried chili pepper
1 Tbsp minced garlic
1 tsp minced ginger
1 tsp fish sauce
1 tsp soy sauce
1 tsp toasted sesame oil

1 To prepare the greens: Soak the greens in a big bowl of water and wash well to remove any dirt from the leaves. Depending on the type of greens you're using, if needed, cut them into smaller pieces and trim any dry, tough stem ends.

2 In a wok or frying pan over high heat, warm the oil until almost smoking. Add the chili pepper, garlic, and ginger and stir-fry quickly for 30 seconds. Add the greens and stir-fry for about 1 minute, until cooked but still green.

3 Add the fish sauce and soy sauce and stir to ensure the ingredients are thoroughly seasoned. Stir in the sesame oil at the very end, remove the wok from the heat, transfer the vegetables to a platter, and serve immediately.

VARIATION

To make a few more spicy and flavorful versions: Prepare the greens and after stir-frying with the chili pepper, garlic, and ginger, add 2 Tbsp / 30ml of Chili Furu Sauce (page 228), Sichuan XO Sauce (page 225), or Ginger-Scallion Chili Sauce (page 228) to the wok. Stir to ensure everything is thoroughly seasoned, remove the wok from the heat, and serve immediately.

CHILI CRISP VINAIGRETTE CABBAGE

This recipe is inspired by a dish I loved growing up: culiu baicai, or napa cabbage in vinegar sauce. It's a dish popular in Eastern China, where my mother's family came from, and it was a favorite of her repertoire at home. I've added a Sichuan twist to it, while maintaining its essential sour flavor profile with chili crisp vinaigrette, and it's one of the tastiest ways to consume cabbage. You can use any type of cabbage here like white, green, or napa, and it's a perfect side dish to go with rice. _Makes 4 servings_

1 tsp cornstarch
¼ cup / 60ml Chili Crisp Vinaigrette (page 226)
1 Tbsp neutral oil
½ tsp whole Sichuan pepper
2 or 3 dried chili peppers
2 tsp minced garlic
1 tsp minced ginger
1 lb / 450g cabbage, cut into bite-size wedges

1 In a small bowl, mix the cornstarch and chili vinaigrette together. Set aside.

2 In a wok over high heat, warm the oil until almost smoking. Add the Sichuan pepper and chili peppers and stir-fry quickly for 30 seconds to release their fragrance. Add the garlic and ginger and stir-fry for another 30 seconds.

3 Add the cabbage and stir-fry for 2 to 3 minutes, until the leaves start to soften. Then add the vinaigrette mixture and continue to stir for about 1 minute, until the sauce has thickened. Remove the wok from the heat, transfer the cabbage and sauce to a serving dish, and serve hot.

CHILI PANEER

At a dinner party I cohosted with my friend Sana, the founder of single-origin Indian spice company Diaspora, we combined the flavor profiles of our cuisines as an ode to Indo-Chinese foodways that developed throughout history via migration patterns along the Silk Road. The origin of Indian Chinese food is said to have centered around Hakka Chinese immigrants in Kolkata hundreds of years ago. These settlers cooked the flavors of their homeland and adapted the spices and ingredients available to them. The resulting cuisine spread like wildfire across India, where you can now find Indo-Chinese food readily. One of the most iconic dishes that came out of this marriage of flavor is chili paneer: crispy, chewy chunks of pan-fried cheese with a sweet and spicy chili sauce. You can make your own paneer, or you can buy it online. I like the versions by Sach Foods that you can find online or in most Whole Foods Markets. _Makes 4 servings_

BATTER
3 Tbsp cornstarch
3 Tbsp all-purpose flour
¼ tsp kosher salt
⅛ tsp Ground Roasted
   Sichuan Pepper
   (page 218)
3 Tbsp water, or as
   needed

SAUCE
1 Tbsp light soy sauce
2 Tbsp Sichuan Chili
   Crisp (page 220)
2 Tbsp tomato paste
1 tsp black vinegar
1 tsp granulated sugar
1 tsp sesame seeds

3 to 4 Tbsp neutral oil
1 cup / 200g paneer, cut
   into ½-inch / 1.3cm
   cubes

2 scallions, green parts
   only, sliced on the
   diagonal

1   To make the batter: In a medium bowl, combine the cornstarch, flour, salt, and roasted Sichuan pepper. Pour in the water and whisk to form a smooth batter, adding more water as needed to keep the consistency smooth.

2   To make the sauce: In a small bowl, mix the soy sauce, chili crisp, tomato paste, vinegar, sugar, and sesame seeds together. Set aside.

3   In a large nonstick pan over medium heat, warm the oil. Dip the paneer cubes in the batter and immediately transfer to the pan, frying and turning the cubes until the cheese is evenly golden brown on each side, 2 to 3 minutes. When all the cubes have been fried, pour the sauce into the pan and stir-fry for about 2 minutes to coat the paneer. The sauce should reduce a bit and shine and glisten.

4   Remove the pan from the heat, transfer the paneer and sauce to a serving bowl, and top with the scallions.

FLY RESTAURANTS:
The Soul of Chengdu

Chengdu, the city where I was born, has provided me with endless inspiration through its flavors and energy. This is a city that's ever changing. It's known throughout the world for its vibrant and dynamic food culture, so much so that it is one of only a handful of cities in the world awarded the coveted UNESCO City of Gastronomy title. Restaurants and food trends change at an alarming rate in Chengdu, but what has remained consistent is the attitude of its people: laid back, playful, and quick to smile.

Fly restaurants, which I wax poetic about at any given chance, is the name given to hole-in-the-wall restaurants in Chengdu that are hidden and run down but are so delicious they're said to attract people like flies. They're an essential lens through which to experience Chengdu's food culture and an extension of the foundation on which the city's culinary tradition is based: street snacks and homestyle cooking. They can be hard to find, usually tucked away down an alley or behind a corner, often without an address. Walls streaked with years of blackened grease and rickety stools and tables spilling onto the sidewalk are the backdrop to eye-poppingly delicious dishes, passed down and honed over generations.

A place that my mother went to as a child still serves the same thick, chewy strands of tianshuimian (sweet-water noodle), bathed in an elixir of chili oil, sweet soy, garlic, and sesame paste. A wooden cart with no name parked by a redbrick wall outside an elementary school still serves the same light and fluffy egg pancake, danhonggao, stuffed with spicy stewed pork and pickled radish. A stall on a busy street corner still kneads bits of ground pork and beef, spiced with Sichuan pepper and salt into a flaky, chewy flatbread called guokui, which is then fried to a golden crisp on a griddle. Hidden inside a residential compound, a gem named Dry Chili Wontons and known for its eponymous dish, may be impossibly hard to find, but never underestimate the crowds of "flies" that flock here for tasty handmade wontons churned out of a tiny apartment kitchen. These, and many more, are the lifeblood of Chengdu's culinary landscape.

Fly restaurants best exemplify the attitude of the Chengdu people: no matter who you are or what you do, for a brief moment, everybody is hunkered down at the same tables, pressed back-to-back with neighbors, and united in the common pursuit of a delicious meal. Flavor trumps everything around here, and appreciating good food is a part of mastering the art of living.

Locals discovered these homestyle eateries in much the same way you or I might, by wandering their neighborhoods, getting lost, and stumbling upon a gem. If you make it to Chengdu, I encourage you to do the same. You'll be amazed at what you'll find.

164 Collagen Congee
167 Dace Fried Rice
168 Chilled Sesame Noodles
171 Dan Dan Noodles
172 Sweet Water Noodles
174 Sichuan Cacio e Pepe
175 Hot and Sour Sweet Potato Noodles
177 Spicy Scallion Oil Noodles
178 Biang Biang Noodles
181 Mapo Ragu with Hand-Pulled Noodles

RĪCE AND NOODLES

COLLAGEN CONGEE

I know that I'm becoming my mother when I start to crave all the things she loved to eat that I always found boring growing up. As a kid, I resisted eating congee. I think that's because I had yet to discover the world of condiments that accompany it and as such, found it bland. As I grew up and visited home, I came to look forward to the warm bowls of congee I knew would greet me every morning along with my mother's homemade salted duck eggs, pickled radishes, and chili sauces. Now I regularly make congee for myself, and my fridge is filled to the brim with jars and bottles of pickled and preserved accoutrements, to the point where there's barely space for fresh food. For a gut-healthy and collagen-rich version, I use bone broth to cook my congee, but you can also just use water. Freezing the rice breaks it up and makes for a much faster cooking time, but if you haven't prepared it the night before, you can cook it low and slow or use an electric rice cooker with a congee setting. You can also add your choice of protein such as shredded chicken, sliced fish, pork, or beef to the cooking process. I always add a ton of vegetables for an easy way to get in my greens. And for the most important part, the toppings, know that anything you like can go here. Frankly, you can eat your congee plain, and it will still be good, but my rule of thumb is to have a crunchy element, a spicy element, a savory element, and some aromatics. For crunch, you can do fried peanuts, or any type of pickles. For spice, chili crisp. For saltiness, fermented tofu, salted duck eggs, or fish sauce. For aromatics, slivered ginger, scallion, or cilantro. With all of this going on, you're guaranteed a flavor adventure with every bite. _Makes 6 servings_

1 cup / 200g white rice
4 cups / 950ml bone
   broth
5 cups / 1.2L water
1 lb / 450g Swiss chard,
   chopped

TOPPINGS
Fermented tofu
Toasted sesame oil
White pepper
Sichuan Chili Crisp
   (page 220)
Sichuan XO Sauce
   (page 225)
Soy sauce
Fish sauce
Pickled mustard tuber
Salted duck eggs
Fried peanuts
Slivered ginger
Scallions
Chopped cilantro leaves

1 Rinse the rice and soak in water for about 30 minutes. Drain and transfer to a sealed container or freezer bag and freeze overnight.

2 In a large pot over high heat, add the broth, water, and frozen rice and bring to a boil. Turn down the heat to medium low and simmer, covered, for about 15 minutes.

3 Increase the heat to medium high, add the chard to the pot, and stir the rice until it thickens and the chard has wilted, about 5 minutes.

4 Serve in individual serving bowls and add your toppings of choice. My favorites are fermented tofu, pickled mustard tuber, salted duck eggs, scallions, cilantro, and chili crisp, of course.

DACE FRIED RICE

Growing up, a pantry mainstay in my house was a tin of Eagle Coin preserved dace fish with salted black beans, bearing its unmistakable yellow and red label. It was one of the few Chinese brands that was widely available at Chinese markets in Europe and Canada, and it was one of my mom's favorite condiments for congee. It's made with fillets of dace fish that have been dried and preserved in oil and is flavored with preserved black beans. It has a mild but deeply umami flavor that lends itself well to stir-fries, too. I started using it to make fried rice at my supper clubs in Shanghai, and this dish became one of my most popular. It pairs especially well with mapo tofu. *Makes 4 or 5 servings*

4 cups / 800g cooked white rice
1 (6.5 oz / 184g) tin Eagle Coin fried dace with salted black beans
2 eggs, whisked
2 Tbsp neutral oil
3 or 4 scallions, green and white parts, sliced, plus more green parts for garnish
1 Tbsp fish sauce
1 tsp kosher salt
1 tsp granulated sugar
Chopped cilantro leaves for serving

1   Prepare the dace by first removing the fillets from the can, one by one. Open the fillet halves to find and discard any bones. Dice the fish into ¼-inch / 6mm chunks and add to a medium bowl along with the oil and the black beans from the can.

2   In a small pan over medium heat, stirfry the whisked eggs for about 1 minute, until set but still soft. Set aside.

3   Pour the oil into a large wok over high heat. Add the scallion whites and diced fish and stir-fry until fragrant. Then add the cooked rice, using a spatula to break apart any clumps. Add the fish sauce, salt, and sugar, stir-frying to ensure the seasoning coats all the ingredients evenly. Add the egg and fry for a few more minutes, mixing it well with the rice.

4   Top with a generous heap of sliced scallion greens and cilantro, transfer to a serving dish, and serve immediately.

CHILLED SESAME NOODLES

Chilled sesame noodles are the perfect summer picnic or potluck food. They're easy to prepare and can be made well in advance. There are really hundreds of variations of this dish, and there are no rules. You can use any type of noodles you like, including rice noodles and Korean japchae, but I prefer using wheat noodles because they tend to have a more toothsome bite. Roasted sesame paste or peanut butter will thicken the sauce and coat the noodles nicely but can be omitted if you'd like a lighter version. *Makes 4 servings*

1 lb / 450g Chinese
   noodles
1 Tbsp neutral oil

1 cucumber, julienned
   into batons 2 inches /
   5cm long
2 tsp kosher salt

SAUCE
3 Tbsp Sichuan Chili
   Crisp (page 220)
3 Tbsp roasted sesame
   paste or peanut butter
3 Tbsp light soy sauce
1½ Tbsp black vinegar
1 tsp toasted sesame oil
1 Tbsp granulated sugar
2 Tbsp minced garlic
¼ tsp Ground Roasted
   Sichuan Pepper
   (page 218)

GARNISHES
Roasted sesame seeds
Sliced scallions, green
   parts only
Chopped cilantro leaves

1   To cook the noodles: In a medium pot over high heat, bring water to a boil and cook the noodles according to the package instructions until they're al dente. (Cooking time will vary based on your choice of noodles.) Drain the noodles in a colander and rinse under cold water to stop them from cooking further.

2   Transfer the noodles to a large bowl and add the neutral oil, mixing to prevent the noodles from sticking together. Set aside.

3   Place the cucumbers in a medium bowl, sprinkle with the salt, and gently massage the cucumbers with your hands to coat. Set aside for at least 15 minutes to lightly pickle and let the water sweat out. Drain the liquid. The cucumbers should taste well seasoned and just slightly crunchy.

4   To make the sauce: In a small bowl, combine the chili crisp, sesame paste, soy sauce, vinegar, sesame oil, sugar, garlic, and roasted Sichuan pepper and mix well. Add 1 to 2 Tbsp of water to dilute the sauce if you want a slightly looser consistency.

5   Place the cucumbers in the bowl with the noodles, pour the sauce over it, and, using tongs, mix well to combine.

6   Transfer the noodles to a serving bowl and garnish with the sesame seeds, scallions, and cilantro.

DAN DAN NOODLES

Happiness for me is slurping a deep bowl of these classic noodles—they're an iconic Sichuan street food dish for a reason! They rose to fame in Chengdu, where they were sold by street hawkers, who carried their wares in baskets tied to bamboo poles (called dan in Chinese); hence, their namesake. Because they're so famous, there are countless variations that have evolved from the original, from Taiwanese to Japanese versions. The beauty of these noodles is that they're delicious no matter what, but these are the dan dan noodles I know.

An essential ingredient in dan dan noodles is yacai, preserved mustard greens. They add the necessary deep umami funk and crunch that make dan dan noodles so addictive. Yibin Suimi Yacai is the brand to get, but it can be hard to find. Try your local Chinese grocery store or search online. If you absolutely cannot find it, you can do without it. *Makes 4 servings*

MEAT TOPPING
Neutral oil for frying
2 Tbsp Yibin Suimi Yacai
¼ lb / 115g ground beef
 or pork
1 tsp light soy sauce
1 tsp dark soy sauce

SAUCE
4 Tbsp Sichuan Chili
 Crisp (page 218)
2 Tbsp light soy sauce
2 Tbsp dark soy sauce
1 tsp Ground Roasted
 Sichuan Pepper
 (page 218), plus more
 for garnish
4 Tbsp thinly sliced
 scallions, green parts
 only, plus more for
 garnish

1 lb / 450g dried thin
 Chinese wheat
 noodles or noodles of
 your choice

1   To make the topping: In a wok over high heat, warm the oil until very hot. Add the suimi yacai and stir-fry for 1 minute, until fragrant. Add the ground meat and both soy sauces and cook for 5 to 6 minutes, until the meat is brown but not dry.

2   To make the sauce: In a small bowl, combine the chili crisp, both soy sauces, roasted Sichuan pepper, and scallions. Divide the sauce evenly into four small bowls.

3   To cook the noodles: In a medium pot over high heat, bring water to a boil and cook the noodles according to the package instructions. Drain the noodles in a colander and rinse under cold water to stop them from cooking further.

4   When ready to serve, divide the noodles among the four bowls with the sauce and top with the ground meat. Garnish with the scallions and a dash of roasted Sichuan pepper.

SWEET WATER NOODLES

In Chengdu, there's a legendary noodle shop across from Wenshu Temple, an ancient Confucian monastery. The star dish of this shop is what's known as sweet water noodles: thick strands of chewy, al dente, freshly pulled noodles, bathed in a sweet, spicy, nutty, and garlicky elixir. With similar notes to the Zhong dumpling sauce, this one is slightly thicker, featuring a slick of roasted sesame paste that somehow transforms it into something else entirely.
Makes 4 servings

SWEET WATER NOODLES
2 cups / 250g high-
    gluten flour plus more
    for dusting
½ cup / 120ml water, or
    as needed
1 tsp kosher salt

¾ cup / 175ml Zhong
    Sesame Dressing
    (page 227)
Sesame seeds for
    garnish

1   To make the noodles: On a large floured work surface, combine the flour, water, and salt to form a dough. Depending on where you live and the level of humidity, you may need to add a bit more water. If you're finding the dough difficult to bring together, slowly add small amounts of water, so the dough doesn't become too wet. You want it to be smooth but not sticky. Wrap the ball of dough in plastic wrap and let it sit at room temperature for 30 to 60 minutes.

2   Unwrap and divide the dough into two pieces. Roll out each piece to a rectangular shape about ⅜ inch / 1cm thick. Cover with plastic wrap for 15 to 20 minutes. Using a knife, cut the pieces lengthwise into ⅜-inch-wide / 1cm sticks.

3   At this point, the dough should be relaxed enough to work with. If it isn't, give it a few more minutes before you take each piece and start to gently pull on each strand. Test the elasticity as you pull—it should extend easily and at least triple in length. If it doesn't, let it rest some more. Pull every strand and set aside on a large sheet pan or other surface, making sure to dust the surface and noodles generously with flour to prevent them from sticking. The strands should be uniform and about ⅛ inch / 3mm thick (they will get thicker after they cook).

4   In a large pot over high heat, bring some very salted water to a boil. Add the noodles in two or three batches so as not to crowd the pot and immediately stir so the strands don't stick together. Boil the noodles for about 5 minutes. When the noodles float to the top, wait an extra minute before taking out one strand to see if it's cooked all the way through. A fully cooked noodle will not have any white raw dough in the center and should taste cooked through but still be al dente.

5   Drain the noodles in a colander and rinse under cold water to stop them from cooking further. You can serve the noodles warm right away or set aside and serve later at room temperature.

6   When ready to serve: Divide the sauce evenly into four large bowls. Portion the noodles equally among the bowls on top of the sauce. Garnish with the sesame seeds.

SICHUAN CACIO E PEPE

This recipe marries two of my favorite things, sweet water noodles and cacio e pepe. It features the al dente chew of the hand-pulled noodles and combines it with the rich, cheesy body of the cacio e pepe sauce. I love to use an ample amount of Diaspora Co's aranya pepper here, and of course, the zing of tribute pepper takes the dish to a whole new dimension. _Makes 4 servings_

1 recipe Sweet Water Noodles (page 172), or 8 oz / 225g store-bought pasta (such as spaghetti or bucatini)

SAUCE
2 Tbsp unsalted butter
½ cup / 120ml reserved noodle water
2 tsp ground black peppercorns, or as needed
2 tsp Ground Roasted Sichuan Pepper (page 218), or as needed
½ cup / 30g finely grated Pecorino Romano, or as needed
½ cup / 15g finely grated Parmigiano-Reggiano, or as needed

1 About an hour before serving, prepare the noodle dough and cook as directed, reserving ½ cup / 120ml noodle water in a bowl. Set the noodles and noodle water aside.

2 To make the sauce: In a large pan or skillet over medium heat, melt the butter. Add the ground black pepper and roasted Sichuan pepper and cook for about 1 minute, until toasted and fragrant.

3 Decrease the heat to low and add the sweet noodles to the pan. Add the reserved noodle water and the grated cheeses and continue to toss until the cheeses have melted.

4 Transfer to a serving plate and top with more cheese, ground black pepper, and roasted Sichuan pepper, if desired.

HOT AND SOUR SWEET POTATO NOODLES

I know I sound like a broken record at this point as every recipe in this book is my favorite, but I can definitely say that suanlafen, or hot and sour sweet potato noodles, is the dish I crave the most on a consistent basis. Piping hot bowls of suanlafen are often served as a snack along with a beef guokui (page 91) at street-side stalls in Chengdu, and something about that combination is irresistible to me. The sweet potato noodles are slippery and chewy and are submerged in an addictive broth, seasoned with chili oil, black vinegar, and aromatics. Try to find sweet potato noodles from Sichuan at your local Asian market. I find they are usually more toothsome than their Korean counterparts like japchae and make for a more satisfying bite. _Makes 2 servings_

4 oz / 115g dried sweet
   potato noodles

SAUCE
2 Tbsp pickled mustard
   stems
2 Tbsp finely chopped
   celery
2 tsp minced garlic
1 tsp minced ginger
2 Tbsp Sichuan Chili
   Crisp (page 220)
1½ Tbsp black vinegar
1 Tbsp soy sauce
1 tsp toasted sesame oil
½ tsp granulated sugar
¼ tsp kosher salt
¼ tsp ground white
   pepper
¼ tsp Ground Roasted
   Sichuan Pepper
   (page 218)

2½ cups / 590ml chicken
   or vegetable stock
¼ cup / 50g bean
   sprouts

GARNISHES
2 Tbsp roasted peanuts
Scallions, green parts
   only, sliced
Chopped cilantro leaves

1   In a medium pot over high heat, bring water to a boil. Add the noodles and cook according to the package instructions. I like mine cooked through but slightly al dente. Drain the noodles in a colander and rinse under cold water to stop them from cooking further. Set aside.

2   To make the sauce: Place the pickled mustard stems, celery, garlic, ginger, chili crisp, vinegar, soy sauce, sesame oil, sugar, salt, white pepper, and roasted Sichuan pepper in a large bowl and mix well. Divide the sauce between two serving bowls.

3   In a small pot over high heat, bring the stock to a boil. Blanch the bean sprouts in the broth until they start to appear translucent, about 2 minutes. Using tongs, transfer the sprouts to the two serving bowls. Using tongs or chopsticks, divide the cooled noodles between the two bowls.

4   Remove the boiling stock from the heat and pour it evenly into the noodle bowls. Top with the peanuts, scallions, and cilantro.

SPICY SCALLION OIL NOODLES

While living in Shanghai, I came to love the surprisingly simple scallion oil noodles that hail from the region. It was astounding to me how much flavor could be packed into a small bowl of wheat noodles with just some fried scallions, soy sauce, and sugar. My only gripe with it was that it lacked the heat I craved with every meal—the Shanghainese like a sweeter flavor profile and rarely cook with chilies—so I make my version with chili oil, and it's become my go-to noodle snack. *Makes 4 to 6 servings*

1½ cups / 150g scallions (6 or 7), green and white parts only
⅓ cup / 80ml Chili Oil (page 219)
3 Tbsp light soy sauce
3 Tbsp dark soy sauce
1.5 oz / 50g rock sugar, or 4 tsp granulated sugar

1 lb / 450g thin Chinese noodles

1 Cut the scallions into 3-inch / 7.5cm segments, then slice lengthwise into thinner strips.

2 In a large pan over medium heat, warm the chili oil. Add the scallions and cook for 5 to 6 minutes, stirring continuously, until they start to become golden brown and crispy. Using tongs, transfer the scallions to a plate and set aside.

3 To the pan of chili oil, add the light and dark soy sauces and the sugar. Simmer the mixture until the sugar is melted, about 3 minutes. Transfer the sauce to either a large bowl (if serving the noodles family style) or divide it evenly among individual small bowls.

4 When ready to serve, in a medium pot over high heat, bring water to a boil. Cook the noodles according to the package instructions. Drain the noodles in a colander.

5 Place the hot noodles into the serving bowl or the individual bowls, mix well with the sauce, and top with the crispy scallions.

BIANG BIANG NOODLES

Biang biang noodles hail from Shaanxi Province and have been made famous in North America in recent years by Xi'an Famous. These are some of the easiest noodles to make from scratch, and you don't have to worry about how they look. The scragglier the strands, the more they will latch onto the flavorful sauce. The basic noodle sauce consists of chili oil, soy sauce, black vinegar, salt, and sugar, with a medley of aromatics and ground spices that are bloomed with hot oil right before serving. For another delicious option: replace the chili oil sauce with ½ cup / 120ml of Chili Furu Sauce (page 228). *Makes 2 servings*

NOODLE DOUGH
2 cups / 250g all-purpose or bread flour, plus more for dusting
½ cup / 120ml water, at room temperature, or as needed
1 tsp kosher salt
Neutral oil for oiling the dough

SAUCE
3 Tbsp soy sauce
2 Tbsp Sichuan Chili Crisp (page 220)
1½ Tbsp black vinegar
1 tsp granulated sugar

FOR SERVING
2 small garlic cloves, minced
1 tsp minced ginger
1 scallion, green and white part only, thinly sliced
1 tsp Ground Chili Powder (page 218)
½ tsp ground cumin
½ tsp ground coriander
½ tsp kosher salt
¼ cup / 60ml neutral oil

1. To make the dough: In a stand mixer fitted with the dough hook, blend the flour, water, and salt on medium speed until a dough comes together, 8 to 10 minutes. You may need to add more water by the teaspoon to form a firm but uniform dough. Transfer the dough to a lightly floured surface and knead until smooth, about 4 minutes. Form the dough into a flat rectangular shape, wrap it in plastic, and let the dough rest at room temperature for 1 to 2 hours.

2. On a lightly floured surface, cut the dough into five equal pieces. Using a rolling pin, roll out each piece into an oval shape, around ¼ inch / 6mm thick. Brush oil on top of each piece of dough, stack them on top of each other, wrap them together in plastic wrap, and let the dough rest at room temperature for 30 minutes or up to 2 hours.

3. Working with one piece of dough at a time and keeping the rest covered, make an indent with a chopstick vertically on the dough to mark the center. Taking both ends with your fingers, gently pull the dough and swing with your arms, allowing the middle part of the noodle to slap the work surface with each swing. After the noodle has tripled in length, pull from the center of the noodle to lengthen and thin it out but take care not to pull it apart—this should be one long connected strand of noodle. Keep bouncing the noodle for a few more seconds. Set the noodle down on a lightly floured work surface and repeat with the rest of the dough.

4. To make the sauce: Combine the soy sauce, chili crisp, vinegar, and sugar in a large serving bowl. Set aside.

5. In a large pot over high heat, bring some salted water to a boil. Drop in the noodles in 2 to 3 batches, give them a stir, and cook until they rise to the top, 2 to 3 minutes. Drain the noodles in a colander and transfer them to the serving bowl with the sauce. Top with the garlic, ginger, scallions, ground chili, cumin, coriander, and salt. Do not stir and set aside.

6. In a small saucepan over medium-high heat, warm the oil until it reaches 275°F / 135°C on an instant-read thermometer. Pour the oil over the noodles and stir all the ingredients together until evenly blended. Serve immediately.

RICE AND NOODLES

MAPO RAGU WITH HAND-PULLED NOODLES

I can never run out of things to put mapo on; its savory, velvety texture begs for a canvas and though I love an accompaniment of freshly steamed rice, it also makes a perfect umami-rich ragu for a pasta sauce. I like to use ground wagyu or pork for an extra decadent fragrance and flavor, but you can also use firm tofu crumbles instead of ground meat if you'd like this dish to be vegan. It works beautifully with the hand-pulled noodles in the recipe for biang biang noodles, but it can also be used on any store-bought pasta and can be made in big batches ahead of time and frozen in an airtight container for up to three months. _Makes 2 servings_

1 recipe biang biang
   noodle dough (see
   page 178), or 4 oz /
   115g store-bought
   pasta

SAUCE
1 Tbsp neutral oil
½ lb / 225g ground beef
   or pork
¼ cup / 60ml Chili Oil
   (page 219)
1 Tbsp minced garlic
1 Tbsp minced ginger
2 Tbsp doubanjiang
2 Tbsp Sichuan Chili
   Crisp (page 220)
1 cup / 240ml bone broth
   (can substitute with
   vegetable stock)
½ cup / 130g tomato
   paste
2 tsp light soy sauce
2 tsp granulated sugar
2 tsp cornstarch
2 Tbsp cold water

2 scallions green parts
   only, thinly sliced, for
   garnish
¼ tsp Ground Roasted
   Sichuan Pepper
   (page 218) for garnish

1   Several hours before serving, prepare the noodle dough, but do not cook the noodles. Set the noodles aside.

2   To make the sauce: In a wok over high heat, warm the neutral oil. Add the ground meat and stir-fry for 4 to 5 minutes, until fully cooked, fragrant, and slightly crisp on the outside. Transfer the meat to a plate and set aside.

3   In the same wok over medium heat, warm the chili oil. Add the garlic and ginger and stir-fry for about 1 minute, until fragrant. Add the doubanjiang and chili crisp and fry for another minute, being careful not to burn the seasonings and aromatics. Add the broth, tomato paste, soy sauce, and sugar and bring the mixture to a boil. Turn down the heat to medium low, add the ground meat back in, and simmer for 7 to 8 minutes.

4   To cook the noodles: While the sauce is simmering, in a large pot over high heat, bring some salted water to a boil. Drop in the noodles, give them a stir, and cook until they rise to the top, 2 to 3 minutes. Drain the noodles in a colander and transfer them to a serving bowl. Top with the sauce mixture and garnish with the scallions and roasted Sichuan pepper.

186 Bingfen "Ice Jelly"
189 Poached Pears in Sichuan Pepper Syrup
190 Brown Sugar Mochi
193 Chili Crisp Sundae with
     Fish Sauce Caramel Brittle
     193   Fish Sauce Caramel Brittle
194 Spicy Almond Butter Cookies
197 Salt and Sichuan Pepper Walnut Cookies
198 Spiced Sticky Date Cake

SWEETS

BINGFEN "ICE JELLY"

Bingfen, or ice jelly, is a ubiquitous street snack on hot summer days in Chengdu, often served with a brown sugar syrup and topped with fresh and dried fruit, nuts, and candies. Bingfen is traditionally made from the seeds of the shoo-fly plant, which is said to have cooling properties, and because of that, bingfen is often served during the summer months and as a side dish at hot pot restaurants. It can be hard to find bingfen outside of China, but because it doesn't have a discernible flavor, konjac is an acceptable substitute for its slippery, Jell-O-like texture. This part is optional, but I love to mix flower teas into my bingfen mixture, as it makes for a beautiful dish once the jelly sets. Drizzle brown sugar syrup over it and add your choice of toppings, and you have the makings of a light and refreshing dessert. _Makes 6 servings_

1 package (about 4¼ oz / 125g) konjac powder
2 Tbsp dried floral tea (optional)
2¼ cups / 540ml hot water
¼ cup / 80g dark brown sugar, lightly packed

TOPPINGS
Boba
Chopped haw flakes
Coconut jelly
Diced dragon fruit
Diced mango
Diced watermelon
Mochi
Roasted peanuts

1   In a large bowl, add the konjac powder and tea. Slowly pour in 2 cups / 480ml of the hot water while stirring to prevent any clumps from forming. Stir until fully mixed, cover, and let cool in the refrigerator for at least 3 hours.

2   In a small pot or saucepan over medium heat, combine the brown sugar with the remaining ¼ cup / 60ml hot water and stir to dissolve the sugar, 1 to 2 minutes. Remove from the heat and let cool.

3   When ready to serve, use a wide spoon to scoop the bingfen into individual serving bowls, add 1 Tbsp of brown sugar syrup or more to taste, and garnish with your desired toppings.

POACHED PEARS IN SICHUAN PEPPER SYRUP

A wonderfully simple, classic Sichuan dessert, this dish showcases the floral flavor of Sichuan pepper and is the perfect ending to a meal, especially when served with some ice cream or a spongy olive oil cake. _Makes 4 servings_

4 cups / 950ml water
1 cup / 200g granulated
    sugar
2 or 3 star anise
1 cinnamon stick
2 (1-inch / 2.5cm) pieces
    ginger, sliced
1 tsp whole Sichuan
    pepper
4 pears, halved
Ice cream or cake for
    serving

1 In a wok over medium heat, bring the water to a simmer. Add the sugar and stir until dissolved. Add the star anise, cinnamon stick, ginger, Sichuan pepper, and the pears. Decrease the heat to medium low and continue to simmer. Cook, covered, for 20 to 25 minutes, until the pears are translucent in color. Using a slotted spoon, transfer the pears to an airtight container and set aside.

2 Increase the heat to medium high and bring the poaching liquid to a boil. Reduce the sauce by about half, until you have a thick syrup, then pour it over the pears. Cool to room temperature.

3 Keep the pears in a container in the refrigerator until ready to serve. If you'd like to serve them warm, you can reheat them gently in their poaching liquid. Or you can serve them chilled with your choice of ice cream or cake.

BROWN SUGAR MOCHI

Ciba, or sticky rice cake, is Sichuan's version of the brown sugar mochi that is ubiquitous in so many Asian food cultures. This is usually made from heavily pounding steamed sticky rice until it forms a cake, but as my lazy self has found, it can also be made with glutinous rice flour and a microwave. This version is rolled in kinako, roasted soybean powder that you can find in Japanese and Korean grocery stores, but if you'd like, you can deep-fry the rice cakes for added texture and flavor. *Makes 4 servings*

1 cup / 140g glutinous
  rice flour, plus more
  for dusting
1 Tbsp granulated sugar
¾ cup plus 6 Tbsp /
  265ml water
6 Tbsp dark brown sugar
2 Tbsp kinako

1   In a large microwave-safe bowl, add the flour, sugar, and ¾ cup / 175ml of the water. Whisk well to combine. Cover with plastic wrap and microwave on high heat for 2 minutes. Remove the bowl from the microwave and, using a spatula, mix the batter and pound it for about 5 minutes to remove any clumps, until the batter is smooth, solid, and stretchy. Cover and set aside.

2   In a small pan over medium heat, combine the brown sugar with the remaining 6 Tbsp / 90ml water. Stir until the sugar has completely dissolved, then pour into a small bowl and set aside.

3   Place the kinako in a small bowl.

4   Generously dust a flat work surface with flour, then place the mochi batter on it and massage it to form a long log. Using a knife, cut the log into 1-inch / 2.5cm pieces and, using your hands, form the pieces into balls. Roll and coat each piece in the kinako and place in a serving bowl.

5   When ready to serve, drizzle the brown sugar syrup on top of the mochi.

CHILI CRISP SUNDAE WITH
FISH SAUCE CARAMEL BRITTLE

I first saw chili crisp on ice cream on a billboard advertisement for a Chongqing ice cream shop that depicted glistening bits of chili and oil dripping down a creamy white soft serve. It was 2018, and I was preparing to launch my Sichuan Chili Crisp in the United States via Kickstarter. I poured a spoonful over some store-bought ice cream and gasped at how strange but fitting the combination was. It just worked. The sweet creaminess of ice cream against the savory, crunchy heat of chili crisp intuitively made sense, but the combination still had the power to shock and delight. I reached out to Wanderlust Creamery, my favorite ice cream shop in LA, and planned a special dish for our launch party in the fall of 2018. We served Sichuan Chili Crisp on top of their ube and White Rabbit candy ice cream and introduced this weird and wonderful combo to American palates for the first time. Numerous articles in the *New York Times* and many viral TikToks later, chili crisp on ice cream now seems as natural as peanut butter and jelly, but I still love watching people's minds get blown the first time they try it. Use any good-quality ice cream you can find, add a spoonful of chili crisp, and a crunchy topping. I love this fish sauce caramel nut brittle, but you can also use fried peanuts. *Makes 4 servings*

1 pint ice cream of your choice
¼ cup / 60ml Sichuan Chili Crisp (page 220)
4 pieces Fish Sauce Caramel Brittle (recipe follows)

Scoop the ice cream into individual bowls and top with the chili crisp and caramel brittle.

FISH SAUCE CARAMEL BRITTLE

Makes 2 lb / 900g

12 oz / 340g peanuts or nuts of choice, chopped
2 cups / 400g granulated sugar
1 Tbsp lemon juice
½ cup / 110g butter
2 Tbsp fish sauce
½ tsp baking soda
Flaky salt for sprinkling

Preheat the oven to 350°F / 175°C. Line a sheet pan with parchment paper.

Lay the nuts in a single layer on the prepared pan and toast for about 10 minutes, until golden and fragrant. Set aside.

In a heavy-bottomed medium saucepan over medium-low heat, combine the sugar, lemon juice, butter, and fish sauce. Stir to melt the butter and dissolve the sugar and simmer for about 20 minutes, until a golden-brown caramel forms. When the temperature reaches 300°F / 150°C on an instant-read thermometer, stir in the baking soda. Working quickly as the mixture will start to foam, stir in the nuts and dump the mixture back onto the prepared pan. Spread it out evenly, sprinkle with the salt, and cool for about 30 minutes, until hardened.

Break the brittle into smaller pieces and store in an airtight container at room temperature for up to 2 weeks.

SPICY ALMOND BUTTER COOKIES

Chili crisp goes particularly well with the creaminess of seed and nut butters, both in savory dishes and sweet ones. I love this easy and gluten-free cookie that combines roasted almonds and rich almond butter with the warm heat of chili crisp. It comes together in just minutes and is the perfect afternoon pick-me-up. *Makes 12 cookies*

1 egg
1 cup / 250g well-stirred almond butter
½ cup / 100g dark brown sugar, lightly packed
1 tsp baking soda
1 Tbsp Sichuan Chili Crisp (page 220)
6 oz / 170g roasted almonds, finely chopped

1   Preheat the oven to 350°F / 175°C. Line a baking tray with parchment paper.

2   In a large bowl, whisk the egg. Using a rubber spatula, fold in the almond butter, brown sugar, baking soda, and chili crisp. Mix until well combined, then fold in the almonds.

3   Scoop out 1 to 2 Tbsp of the dough and form a ball. Place on the prepared baking tray and repeat until the dough is finished, leaving about ½ inch / 1.3cm of space between each cookie. You should have enough to form about twelve balls. Press down with the back of a spoon to gently flatten each and bake for 10 to 12 minutes.

4   Remove the tray from the oven and place the cookies on a wire rack to cool. Let the cookies sit for at least 30 minutes before consuming. Store in an airtight container at room temperature for up to 1 week.

SALT AND SICHUAN PEPPER WALNUT COOKIES

These cookies are an ode to one of my favorite treats that my grandparents always kept hand on hand whenever I visited. There aren't a ton of baked confectionaries in Sichuan cuisine, but Gong Ting Bakery is an exception; it has built a cult following for over a hundred years. They churn out quality baked goods with unusual signature flavor profiles, like their famous jiaoyan "salt and Sichuan pepper" walnut cookies that melt right in your mouth. They have an addictive balance of sweet and savory and a lingering tingle of Sichuan pepper. The impossibly crumbly texture is due to the liberal use of lard, and the sweet richness of the cookie is balanced with the salt and Sichuan pepper mixture. *Makes 12 cookies*

4⅓ cups / 540g
   low-gluten flour
1 tsp baking soda
½ tsp baking powder
1 tsp kosher salt
1½ Tbsp Ground
   Roasted Sichuan
   Pepper (page 218)
2 eggs
1⅛ cups / 240g lard
½ cup / 110g unsalted
   butter, room
   temperature
1¼ cups / 240g
   granulated sugar
1½ cups / 140g walnuts,
   finely chopped
1 Tbsp roasted sesame
   seeds

1   In a large bowl, sift together the flour, baking soda, baking powder, salt, and roasted Sichuan pepper. Set aside.

2   In a small bowl, whisk the eggs and reserve 1 Tbsp for later.

3   In a medium bowl, whisk together the lard, butter, sugar, beaten egg (except for that 1 Tbsp), and mix well. Add this wet mixture to the bowl with the dry ingredients along with the walnuts. Using a rubber spatula, combine everything together to form a dough.

4   Preheat the oven to 350°F / 175°C. Line a baking tray with parchment paper.

5   Using your hands, divide the dough into two pieces and keep dividing each half into two more pieces, until you have twelve pieces. Roll each piece into a ball and flatten it slightly with your palms.

6   Place the balls on the prepared tray, leaving about an inch of space between each cookie. Cover in plastic wrap and set the tray aside for about 15 minutes. Brush each cookie with the residual egg mixture and sprinkle some sesame seeds in the center of each one.

7   Bake the cookies for about 20 minutes, until they are golden in color. Remove from the oven and place on a wire rack to cool. Store in an airtight container at room temperature for up to 1 week.

SPICED STICKY DATE CAKE

Despite desserts being relatively uncommon in Sichuan cuisine, I love a sweet ending, especially ones with a little spice. If it's not already obvious, I love turning anything I make into a vessel for spice and Sichuan pepper, so you know I managed to make a spicy version of one of my favorite desserts, sticky date cake. The sweetness of the dates marries perfectly with the heat of the chili. The key here is to buy quality dates and a great low-gluten cake flour. Serve warm with salted caramel ice cream on the side and a drizzle of chili crisp. _Makes 12 servings_

Unsalted butter for greasing the pan
1 lb / 450g fresh soft dates, pitted
2 tsp baking soda
2¼ cups / 530ml very hot water
1 vanilla bean
1½ cups / 300g granulated sugar
1 egg, plus an additional yolk
2 cups / 270g low-gluten cake flour
2 tsp baking powder

SAUCE
2¼ cups / 400g packed dark brown sugar
⅓ cup / 70g unsalted butter
1 cup / 240ml heavy cream
2½ Tbsp whiskey, or as needed
2 tsp ground chili flakes, or as needed
½ tsp Ground Roasted Sichuan Pepper (page 218), or as needed

Ice cream for serving
Sichuan Chili Crisp (optional; page 220)

1   Preheat the oven to 350°F / 175°C. Butter a 10 by 14-inch / 25 by 36cm glass or metal baking dish.

2   In a small bowl, combine the dates and baking soda. Pour the hot water over both and mix with a fork for about 5 minutes, until mostly dissolved and pulpy.

3   In a medium bowl, scrape the seeds from the vanilla bean, add the sugar, egg, and additional yolk, and whisk for about 4 to 5 minutes, until the mixture is pale yellow and creates smooth ribbons when lifted with a spoon. Stir in the date mixture and incorporate completely, about a minute.

4   In a small bowl, sift together the flour and baking powder. Gently fold the flour mixture into the date mixture just until incorporated.

5   Pour the batter into the prepared baking dish and bake until a toothpick inserted in the center comes out clean, 40 to 45 minutes. Turn off the oven and let the cake rest in the oven for 40 minutes.

6   To make the sauce: While the cake is baking, in a large heavy-bottomed saucepan over low heat, stir the brown sugar into the butter, melting the butter and dissolving the brown sugar. As soon as the sugar has dissolved, pour in the cream in a slow and steady stream, whisking constantly. Remove the saucepan from the heat and whisk in the whiskey, chili flakes, and roasted Sichuan pepper. Adjust as necessary to taste.

7   Remove the cake from the oven. Pierce it all over about twenty times with a butter knife and spread half of the sauce over the top, allowing it to seep into the holes on the cake. Set the cake and the remaining sauce aside until ready to serve.

8   When ready to serve, reheat the cake in the oven at 300°F / 150°C and the remaining sauce in a small pan over low heat. Drizzle the remaining sauce on top of the cake and serve with ice cream. Try adding chili crisp to your ice cream as well! The cake can be stored at room temperature in the baking dish covered in plastic wrap for 1 day or in the refrigerator for up to 3 days.

204   Sparkling Berry Shrub
207   Baijiu Negroni
208   Bloody Sichuan Caesar
211   Spicy Paloma
      211   Mala Simple Syrup
212   Mala Margarita

COCKTAILS

SPARKLING BERRY SHRUB

One of the reasons I loved living in China and why I love living in California today is the abundance of fresh fruit and produce that change with the seasons. Spring brings plums and kumquats; summer brings lychees, passionfruit, and figs; and fall and winter bring loquats, persimmons, and dates. It's hard to pick a favorite fruit, but one of the most unique would have to be yangmei, or waxberries, which are crimson, ping-pong ball–shaped fuzzy fruits, bursting with sweet and pleasantly tart juices. Whenever I can find them, I load up and make a shrub to preserve the flavor for months to come. When in season, you can find waxberries at your local Chinese market, but this is a universal shrub recipe that you can use for any ripe fruit. Try using strawberries, rhubarb, plums, or lychees. _Makes 8 to 10 servings_

SYRUP CONCENTRATE
1 lb / 450g waxberries or any in-season fruit
2 cups / 400g granulated sugar
2 cups / 480ml rice vinegar or apple cider vinegar

Sparkling water for serving
Thyme sprig for garnish

1 To make the concentrate: Wash, peel, core, and cut the fruit into smaller pieces.

2 In a medium bowl, combine the fruit with the sugar and use your hands to massage everything together well. Cover the bowl with plastic wrap and refrigerate for at least 24 hours.

3 Strain the syrup through a fine-mesh sieve into a bowl. If there is any sugar that hasn't dissolved, blend it in with a whisk. Whisk in the vinegar and mix well.

4 Transfer to a clean 1-qt / 950ml bottle or jar and keep refrigerated for up to 4 months. To serve, I usually add 1 part concentrate to 4 parts sparkling water and garnish with a sprig of thyme.

BAIJIU NEGRONI

Baijiu, which translates to "white spirits" in Chinese, is one of the oldest liquors in the world. It's distilled from all kinds of grains, from sorghum to corn, wheat, and millet, and is fermented with qu, naturally harvested airborne yeasts that give the liquor a distinct regional style and "terroir." Sichuan has a long tradition of making baijiu and hosts some of the longest-running distilleries in the world. One of them in the town of Luzhou makes one of my favorite brands that's available in the West: Ming River. I love what Ming River is doing to preserve tradition and introduce this ancient art to new generations around the world. We've collaborated on quite a few events together over the years and this cocktail always hits the mark. *Makes 1 serving*

INFUSED CAMPARI
1 tsp whole Sichuan
   pepper
4 oz / 120ml Campari

1 oz / 30ml baijiu
1 oz / 30ml sweet
   vermouth
1 star anise, torched
   with a hand torch
   for garnish

1 To infuse the Campari: Soak the Sichuan pepper in the Campari for 24 hours, and then remove.

2 When ready to serve the cocktail, stir the infused Campari, baijiu, vermouth, and ice in a shaker. Place a large ice cube in a cocktail glass and strain the mixture over the ice cube. Garnish with a torched star anise.

BLOODY SICHUAN CAESAR

Since Canada is my second home, I've always had a love for Bloody Caesars, the cousin of Bloody Marys, made with Clamato juice instead of the classic tomato juice. Given the choice, I will always opt for more umami. My Sichuan twist on it, with soy sauce and chili oil added to the mix and a salt-and-tribute-pepper rim, is not for the faint of heart. *Makes 1 serving*

Salt and Sichuan Pepper
  Seasoning (page 223)
  for rimming the glass
1 to 2 oz / 30 to 60ml
  vodka
4 oz / 120ml Clamato
  juice
½ tsp soy sauce
½ tsp Worcestershire
  sauce
½ tsp Chili Oil
  (page 219)
1 tsp lime juice
Pinch of Ground
  Roasted Sichuan
  Pepper (page 218)
Sichuan Lacto-
  Fermented Pickles
  (page 39) for garnish

1 Coat the rim of a tall glass with salt and tribute pepper seasoning. Fill the glass with ice and set aside.

2 In a shaker, combine the vodka, Clamato juice, soy sauce, Worcestershire sauce, chili oil, lime juice, and roasted Sichuan pepper. Shake well and pour into the prepared glass. Garnish with a stick of fermented pickle.

SPICY PALOMA

I love the way that Sichuan pepper complements citrusy fruit like lemon, yuzu, pomelo, and grapefruit and thought it would be perfect to add a zing to one of my favorite cocktails, a paloma. The mala simple syrup is super quick and easy to make. It can be stored in the refrigerator for up to a month and added to almost any cocktail that calls for a bit of sweetness. _Makes 1 serving_

1 oz / 30ml mezcal
3 oz / 90ml grapefruit
   juice
1 oz / 30ml Mala Simple
   Syrup (recipe follows)
Squeeze of lime
Splash of sparkling water
Chili oil for garnish

In a shaker, combine the mezcal, grapefruit juice, simple syrup, and lime. Shake well and pour over ice in a glass. Top with the sparkling water. Drizzle with a few dots of chili oil on top, and enjoy.

MALA SIMPLE SYRUP

Makes 1 cup / 240ml

1 cup / 240ml water
1 cup / 200g granulated sugar
1 tsp whole Sichuan pepper
2 or 3 pieces dried chilies

In a medium pot over high heat, bring the water to a boil. Add the sugar, stirring to dissolve. Lower the heat, add the Sichuan pepper and chilies, and simmer for about 10 minutes. Remove the pot from the heat and let the syrup cool. Strain the syrup through a fine-mesh sieve into a glass jar to remove the spices. You can use the syrup immediately or store the jar in the refrigerator for up to several weeks.

MALA MARGARITA

I don't know anyone who doesn't enjoy a good margarita, and this version uses a spicy and tingly mala simple syrup that adds beautiful heat and dimension. *Makes 1 serving*

Mala Spice Mix (page 223) for rimming the glass
1 to 2 oz / 30 to 60ml mezcal or tequila
1 oz / 30ml orange liqueur
1 oz / 30ml lime juice
1 oz / 30ml Mala Simple Syrup (page 211)
Lime wedge for garnish

1 Coat the rim of a tall glass with the spice mix. Fill the glass with ice and set aside.

2 In a cocktail shaker, combine the mezcal, orange liqueur, lime juice, simple syrup, and a couple ice cubes. Shake well for about 10 seconds. Strain the margarita through a fine-mesh sieve into the prepared glass, garnish with the lime wedge, and enjoy!

218   Ground Chili Powder
218   Ground Roasted Sichuan Pepper
219   Chili Oil
219   Tribute Pepper Oil
220   Sichuan Chili Crisp
223   Salt and Sichuan Pepper Seasoning
223   Mala Spice Mix
224   Zhong Sauce
        224   Sichuan Sweet Soy Sauce
225   Kungpao Sauce
225   Sichuan XO Sauce
226   Chili Crisp Aioli
226   Chili Crisp Vinaigrette
227   Zhong Sesame Dressing
227   Strange-Flavor Sauce
228   Fish-Fragrant Sauce
228   Ginger-Scallion Chili Sauce
228   Chili Furu Sauce

CONDIMENTS AND SEASONINGS

GROUND CHILI POWDER

You can buy preground chili powder, but like most spices, it loses its potency and luster very quickly. For the best effect, I'd recommend buying whole chilies and toasting them with a bit of oil before you grind them. *Makes ⅓ cup*

1 Tbsp neutral oil
⅓ cup / 50g dried chilies (such as erjingtiao)

Remove the stems of the chilies and cut them into segments.

In a wok or frying pan over medium-low heat, warm the oil. Add the chilies to the pan, stirring for 3 to 4 minutes, until the chilies smell very aromatic and deepen in color to a bright red. Remove the pan from the heat and let cool.

Using a mortar and pestle or a spice grinder, grind the chilies to a powder. It's up to you whether to grind them to a fine powder or leave coarse. You can use the ground chilies for chili oil, stir-fries, or many other recipes in this book. Use immediately or store in an airtight container at room temperature for up to a month.

GROUND ROASTED SICHUAN PEPPER

The best Sichuan pepper is so potent when it's harvested that it's borderline intoxicating, but it loses its potency quickly, especially when not stored properly. If you get your hands on some good-quality Sichuan pepper (at Fly By Jing, we carry a fresh harvest of tribute peppers every year), make sure to store it in the freezer and roast and grind only as much as you need each time to preserve its flavor. *Makes 1 Tbsp*

2 Tbsp whole Sichuan pepper

Heat a wok or frying pan over low heat and add the Sichuan pepper, stirring with a spatula to toast it evenly. Toast for 3 to 4 minutes, making sure not to burn the pepper. Good Sichuan pepper will still have a lot of its oils and fragrance that will be released as you toast it. Remove the wok from the heat and set it aside to cool.

Using a mortar and pestle or a spice grinder, grind the pepper to a fine powder. You'll find that the inner husk of the Sichuan pepper is hard to grind and will be quite visible. Since it doesn't have any flavor, it should ideally be sifted out for the best flavor experience. I usually pass mine through a fine-mesh strainer.

Use the Sichuan pepper immediately.

CHILI OIL

It's hard for me to think of a dish that I don't complement with chili oil. I add it to everything—Sichuan noodles, dumplings, stir-fries, fresh fruit, and ice cream. Chili oil is one of the most rewarding things to make in the Sichuan cooking repertoire because of its ease and versatility. At its base, the ingredients are simple—just oil, aromatics, and ground dried chilies. I add a few other things in there as well to punch up the flavor. The chili I most frequently use is Sichuan's popular erjingtiao variety, but you can mix your own concoction of dried chilies to your preference. Try Korean chili flakes, which tend to be milder, or Mexican chiles de árbol and dried Thai bird's-eye chilies if you want an extra kick of heat. See what you can find online or at your local Asian grocer. If not already ground, you'll need to use a spice grinder to grind up your chilies to a consistency you like. I prefer a medium grind, where you still see bits of skin and seeds. As for the oil, semi-winter rapeseed oil is commonly used in Sichuan for its warm nuttiness and numerous health benefits, but neutral oils with high smoking points, like peanut, soybean, or grapeseed, all work well. *Makes 2 cups*

2 cups / 480ml neutral oil
2 pieces star anise
1 piece cassia bark
1 or 2 pieces cardamom
1 or 2 scallions, white part only, chopped
1 or 2 (1-inch / 2.5cm) pieces ginger, sliced
1 cup / 120g Ground Chili Powder (page 218)
1 tsp sesame seeds

In a wok or frying pan over high heat, warm the oil with the star anise, cassia bark, cardamom, scallions, and ginger, until the spices are bubbling and it reaches 285°F / 140°C on an instant-read thermometer.

In a heatproof bowl or container, combine the chili powder and sesame seeds. Once the oil is at temperature, remove the solids with a slotted spoon or fine-mesh sieve. Slowly pour the oil over the chili powder and stir. You should see and hear a delightful sizzle and immediately smell the release of fragrance from the chili powder.

Once the chili oil has cooled, transfer to an airtight jar and store in a cool, dark place for up to 3 months. You can use the chili oil right away, but it will taste best after sitting for several days.

TRIBUTE PEPPER OIL

Like the tribute pepper itself, a little bit of this oil will go a long way. Use in dishes that call for evenly distributed numbing flavor, like the Celtuce, Vermicelli, and Chicken Salad (page 41). *Makes 1 cup*

1 cup / 240ml neutral oil
2 Tbsp Ground Roasted Sichuan Pepper (page 218)

In a wok or frying pan over high heat, warm the oil to 250°F / 120°C.

Place the roasted Sichuan pepper in a heatproof container. Once the oil is at temperature, slowly pour it over the roasted Sichuan pepper, stirring well. Set aside to cool, then transfer to an airtight jar. You'll want to wait a couple of days before using it, because its flavor will develop over time. Store the jar in a cool, dark place for up to a month.

SICHUAN CHILI CRISP

This is the sauce that started it all. After years of watching my extended family in Sichuan make their homemade versions of chili sauce, each one with a distinct flavor that set it apart from the next, I started mixing my own in my Shanghai kitchen. The technique remained the same: heat oil to 260°F / 125°C, layer in the ingredients, and precisely cook each ingredient until its fragrance is released and the flavors have melded. But it was the ingredients themselves that I had a distinct point of view on. After years of sourcing trips across the Sichuan countryside, I had built relationships with the best of the best purveyors of chilies, tribute peppers, preserved black beans, and more. I felt as if I were weaving the elements of a beautiful story, one that I was helping to tell every time I dolloped a spoonful of chili crisp on a dish. Chili crisp, like anything else, is nothing more than the expression of the ingredients that you put into it. Depending on the type of chilies, oil, and spices that you choose, the flavors will vary. Use the following recipe as a guide to the approximate proportions of each ingredient but be reassured there are no wrong answers. Experiment with chilies of different origins, heat levels, and fragrances to arrive at the right flavor profile for you. *Makes 3 cups*

2 cups / 480ml Sichuan rapeseed or neutral oil
1 piece cassia bark
2 pieces star anise
1 or 2 pieces cardamom
2 Tbsp minced garlic
1 Tbsp minced ginger
¼ cup / 50g preserved black beans
½ cup / 125g Ground Chili Powder (page 218)
2 Tbsp mushroom powder
2⅓ Tbsp kosher salt
2 tsp Ground Roasted Sichuan Pepper
2 Tbsp toasted sesame oil
2 Tbsp fried shallots, store-bought
2 Tbsp fried minced garlic, store-bought

In a large wok or frying pan over high heat, warm the rapeseed oil to 350°F / 175°C on an instant-read thermometer. Add the cassia bark, star anise, and cardamom and fry for 3 to 4 minutes, until their fragrances have been released into the oil. (You'll know when this has happened when the spices stop bubbling in the oil.) Pour the oil through a fine-mesh strainer and discard the spices.

Add the garlic, ginger, and preserved black beans to the oil and fry for 2 to 3 minutes until fragrant. Bring the oil to 260°F / 125°C and add the chili powder, mushroom powder, salt, and roasted Sichuan pepper, stirring to combine and making sure the salt is fully dissolved. Remove the wok from the heat and let the ingredients simmer in the hot oil for a few minutes. Stir in the sesame oil, shallots, and garlic. Allow the mixture to cool.

Transfer the sauce to an airtight container and store at room temperature for up to 6 months or in the refrigerator for up to 12 months. You can use the chili crisp right away, but since the flavor develops over time, you'll find it intensifying after a few days and even more so after a few weeks. Since the solid bits will settle at the bottom, make sure to always mix up the chili oil with a spoon before each use!

SALT AND SICHUAN PEPPER SEASONING

Jiaoyan translates to salt and (Sichuan) pepper and is one of the key flavor profiles in the Sichuan culinary repertoire. This combination finds its way onto cured meats, stir-fries, pastries, and makes a great cocktail rim as well. *Makes 2½ Tbsp*

2 Tbsp kosher salt
1 Tbsp whole Sichuan pepper

In a wok or frying pan over low heat, add the salt and Sichuan pepper. Toast for 3 to 4 minutes, until the Sichuan pepper is fragrant and the salt turns slightly darker in color. Transfer to a mortar and pestle and grind the Sichuan pepper to a powder.

Use immediately or store in an airtight container for up to 1 month.

MALA SPICE MIX

This is the ultimate versatile spice mix, good as a marinade, seasoning, and dry rub or just sprinkled on popcorn. It's no wonder it's one of Fly By Jing's best-selling products. I always have at least a few jars on hand to add oomph to my favorite dishes such as Lazi Chicken Wings (page 15), smashed crispy potatoes (page 150), grilled fish, and roasted sheet pan chicken thighs (page 119). *Makes ½ cup*

⅓ cup / 50g dried erjingtiao chili, cut into
    segments
2 Tbsp cumin seeds
1½ tsp fennel seeds
2 pieces star anise
2 pieces cardamom
1 tsp cloves
3 Tbsp granulated sugar
1 Tbsp kosher salt

In a wok or frying pan over medium-low heat, toast the chili, cumin, fennel, star anise, cardamom, and cloves until fragrant, 3 to 4 minutes. Transfer the mixture to a small bowl and let cool.

Add the sugar and salt to the toasted mixture and mix well. Using a mortar and pestle or a spice grinder, grind the entire mixture until it reaches a fine powder consistency. Use immediately or store in an airtight container for up to 2 weeks.

ZHONG SAUCE

Inspired by my favorite dish growing up, Zhong dumplings, this has become the most popular sauce we sell at Fly By Jing, next to Sichuan Chili Crisp. Sweet, savory, spicy, and filled with umami, it's the perfect accompaniment to so much more than just dumplings. Try it as a glaze on top of roasted salmon (page 111), chicken wings, tofu steaks, meatballs, and brussels sprouts.

Makes 2½ cups

1 cup / 240ml neutral oil
½ cup / 100g minced garlic
⅓ cup / 50g Ground Chili Powder (page 218)
2 Tbsp toasted sesame oil
1 cup / 240ml Sichuan Sweet Soy Sauce
  (recipe follows)

In a wok or frying pan over high heat, warm the neutral oil to 350°F / 175°C. Add the garlic and fry until golden, 3 to 5 minutes.

Bring the oil to 260°F / 125°C on an instant-read thermometer and add the chili powder, stirring well as the chilies release their fragrance and color into the oil. Add the sesame oil and turn off the heat to allow the chili oil to cool down.

Transfer into a medium bowl, combine with the Sichuan sweet soy sauce and mix well. Store in an airtight container in the refrigerator for up to 3 months.

Sichuan Sweet Soy Sauce

Makes 3 cups

2 cups / 480ml light soy sauce
2 cups / 400g dark brown sugar, lightly packed
2 cardamom pods
1 or 2 pieces star anise
1 piece cassia bark
1 (1-inch / 2.5cm) slice ginger
1 tsp fennel seeds
1 bay leaf
1 tsp whole Sichuan pepper

In a medium saucepan over medium-low heat, bring the soy sauce and brown sugar to a simmer. Place the cardamom, star anise, cassia bark, ginger, fennel seeds, bay leaf, and Sichuan pepper in a spice bag. (If you don't have a spice bag, add everything directly to the pot and remember to strain the sauce when it has finished.) Add the spice bag to the pot and adjust the heat to the lowest setting. Simmer for at least 1 hour. Remove the saucepan from the heat and let the sauce steep overnight. Remove the spice bag and store in an airtight container in the refrigerator for up to 3 weeks.

KUNGPAO SAUCE

With this sauce in tow, you'll be able to confidently "kungpao" anything. This is enough for a pound of protein. Some of my favorites include shrimp (page 112), chicken, meatballs (page 127), scallops, mushrooms, and crispy tofu. *Makes ⅓ cup*

2 Tbsp granulated sugar
2 Tbsp chicken stock or water
2 tsp Shaoxing wine
2 tsp light soy sauce
1 tsp dark soy sauce
2 Tbsp black vinegar
½ tsp cornstarch

In a small bowl, mix all ingredients together until well-combined. Transfer to an airtight container and store in the refrigerator for up to 2 weeks. When ready to use, make sure to mix well again before cooking.

SICHUAN XO SAUCE

XO sauce, a rich and layered spicy condiment made by slow-cooking dried seafood and chilies in oil, hails from the Canton region of southern China. It's delicious, packed with umami-rich dried scallop, shrimp, and preserved salted ham, but as you can imagine, it can get pretty expensive. With a bit of time and some high-quality ingredients, you can make your own at home. I like to add doubanjiang for added depth and a Sichuan twist. *Makes 4 cups*

2 cups / 480ml Sichuan rapeseed oil or neutral oil
½ cup / 150g dried scallop, soaked in hot water for 1 to 2 hours
½ cup /150g dried shrimp, soaked in hot water for 1 to 2 hours
6 oz / 170g Jinhua ham or Virginia country ham
½ cup / 100g minced garlic
½ cup / 120g minced shallots
5 bird's-eye chilies, finely diced
2 Tbsp doubanjiang
1 cup / 240ml chicken stock
2 tsp kosher salt
2 Tbsp dark brown sugar, lightly packed
2 Tbsp fish sauce

Finely chop the dried scallop and shrimp.

In a large wok over medium heat, warm the oil to 250°F / 120°C. Add the scallop and fry for about 5 minutes, until golden. Then add the shrimp and ham and fry for another 10 to 15 minutes, until cooked. Add the garlic, shallots, and chilies and cook for another 5 minutes, until their fragrance is released.

Add the doubanjiang, stock, salt, brown sugar, and fish sauce and lower the heat to medium low. Let the ingredients simmer for about an hour and reduce as they cook, stirring every few minutes to avoid any ingredients settling at the bottom and burning.

Once most of the liquid has evaporated and the sauce is the consistency you want, remove the wok from the heat and transfer the sauce to your container of choice. You can consume right away as a topping on rice or other dish, but it will get even better after a few days as the flavors settle in. Store in an airtight container in the refrigerator for up to 3 months.

CHILI CRISP AIOLI

This is a sauce I like to use for sandwiches, potato salads, or mixed with smoked salmon to stuff in an onigiri. You can also use it as a tasty accompaniment for the Wagyu cheeseburger pot stickers (page 87).

Makes ¼ cup

2 Tbsp Sichuan Chili Crisp (page 220)
¼ cup / 60g mayonnaise
1 tsp minced garlic
1 tsp minced ginger
1 Tbsp rice vinegar

In a medium bowl, add the chili crisp, mayonnaise, garlic, ginger, and vinegar. Mix well to combine. Use immediately or store in an airtight container in the refrigerator for up to 5 days.

CHILI CRISP VINAIGRETTE

Chili crisp vinaigrette exemplifies my favorite kind of flavor: compound flavor, which in Sichuanese cuisine demonstrates the delicate balance of multiple flavor profiles dancing in unison. It's the ultimate mother sauce and forms the basis of so many other sauces. I've been mixing some version of this versatile concoction in my kitchen for as long as I can remember, even before I developed Sichuan chili crisp. Different renditions of it make up the foundation of classic Sichuan dishes, from wontons to noodles to salads. In fact, it was the at-home recipe for chili crisp vinaigrette featured in the *New York Times* that catapulted Fly By Jing into mainstream awareness back in 2020. It's a balanced elixir of soy sauce, ten-year-old aged black vinegar, a touch of sweetness, and the unmistakable depth of Sichuan chili crisp, and is my absolute favorite thing to dress dumplings with. But over the years, I've found that there is little that a splash of chili crisp vinaigrette doesn't improve. We make a version at Fly By Jing, but you can make your own below.

Makes ½ cup

3 Tbsp Sichuan Chili Crisp (page 220)
3 Tbsp light soy sauce
1½ Tbsp black vinegar
1 tsp toasted sesame oil
1 tsp honey, or as needed
2 tsp minced garlic
1 scallion, white and green part only, chopped

In a medium bowl, mix the chili crisp, soy sauce, vinegar, sesame oil, honey, garlic, and scallion together. Add more honey for sweetness, if desired. Use immediately or store in an airtight container in the refrigerator for up to 5 days.

ZHONG SESAME DRESSING

When developing the sauces for my Zhong dumplings, I realized the ingredients were remarkably similar to the base sauce for sweet water noodles, with roasted sesame paste being the main addition to the latter. Zhong sauce became my shortcut for making sweet water noodles (page 172), but once you try this sauce, you'll want to put it on everything. Try pouring it over poached Chinese greens, draped over roasted chicken or salmon, or even as a dip for your nuggets.
Makes 1 cup

¾ cup / 175ml Zhong Sauce (page 224)
1 Tbsp minced garlic
¼ cup roasted sesame paste
1 tsp roasted sesame seeds

Combine the Zhong sauce, garlic, sesame paste, and sesame seeds in a bowl and whisk well to combine. You can thin out the sauce a bit if you want a runnier dressing by adding water, a tablespoon at a time, until you reach the consistency you want. Use immediately or store in an airtight container in the refrigerator for up to 1 week.

STRANGE-FLAVOR SAUCE

Named after the famous Sichuan flavor profile characterized by a perfect balance of sweet, spicy, savory, tingly, and nutty, this sauce is a winner on cold poached chicken, noodles, and your next poke bowl.
Makes ¾ cup

⅛ cup / 30ml water
¼ cup / 60g sesame paste
¼ cup / 60ml light soy sauce
¼ cup / 60g Chili Oil (page 219)
1 Tbsp black vinegar
1 Tbsp granulated sugar
2 tsp toasted sesame oil
1 tsp kosher salt
¼ tsp Ground Roasted Sichuan
    Pepper (page 218)

In a medium bowl, add the water to the sesame paste and mix until creamy. Add the soy sauce, chili crisp, vinegar, sugar, sesame oil, salt, and roasted Sichuan pepper and mix well to combine, making sure to completely dissolve the salt and sugar. Store in an airtight container in the refrigerator for up to 2 weeks.

FISH-FRAGRANT SAUCE

Pickled chilies are the star in this sauce, giving a luxurious flavor kick that's warm and slightly sweet and acidic. Pickled chilies are readily available at Asian stores, but substitute with doubanjiang if you can't find them. Despite its name, there is no fish in this sauce, but the flavor profile is meant to evoke fish dishes of similar preparation. Use this sauce to stir-fry eggplant, steamed or deep-fried pork, or seafood. *Makes ½ cup*

2 tsp black vinegar
2 tsp granulated sugar
1 Tbsp light soy sauce
2 Tbsp chicken stock
¼ cup / 60g pickled chili sauce
1 Tbsp minced ginger
1 Tbsp minced garlic
2 Tbsp scallions, green parts only, sliced
1 tsp toasted sesame oil

In a small bowl, mix the vinegar, sugar, soy sauce, stock, chili sauce, ginger, garlic, scallions, and sesame oil together, making sure to completely dissolve all the sugar. Use immediately to top cold appetizers or store in an airtight container in the refrigerator for up to 5 days.

GINGER-SCALLION CHILI SAUCE

A spicy take on one of my favorite condiments for roasted meats, steamed vegetables, and noodles, this ginger-scallion chili sauce is extremely easy to make and is a mainstay in my fridge. *Makes 1½ cups*

1 cup / 240ml neutral oil
¼ cup Ground Chili Powder (page 218)
½ cup / 120g minced ginger
5 or 6 scallions, green and white parts, thinly sliced
1½ tsp kosher salt
1 tsp granulated sugar

In a wok or frying pan over high heat, warm the oil to 260°F / 125°C on an instant-read thermometer. Add the chili powder, ginger, scallions, salt, and sugar and cook for 7 minutes, stirring well. Remove the wok from the heat and set aside to cool. Consume right away or transfer to an airtight container and store in the refrigerator for up to 1 week.

CHILI FURU SAUCE

Furu, or fermented tofu, is my secret ingredient in many dishes. The deep, savory, fermented funk is incredibly flavorful when blended with other elements like sesame paste, soy sauce, and black vinegar. I like to use this sauce on stir-fried morning glory (also known as water spinach), but it's absolutely delicious draped on everything from fried tofu to noodles. *Makes ¾ cup*

1 (5g) block spicy furu
¼ cup / 60g sesame paste
¼ cup / 60ml light soy sauce
2 Tbsp black vinegar
3 Tbsp chicken stock
3 Tbsp granulated sugar
½ Tbsp kosher salt
¼ tsp Ground Roasted Sichuan Pepper (page 218)

In a medium bowl, whisk the furu, sesame paste, soy sauce, vinegar, stock, sugar, salt, and roasted Sichuan pepper together until smooth. Use immediately or store in an airtight container in the refrigerator for up to 5 days.

About the Contributors

JING GAO, the founder and CEO of Fly By Jing, is a chef, entrepreneur, and renowned expert on Chinese cuisine, whose mission is to bring uncensored Chinese flavors to the table. She was born in Chengdu but grew up everywhere, and she uses her experience as a chef to share meaningful flavors that open up people to new ideas and conversations. She was the founder of an award-winning, modern-Chinese, fast-casual restaurant in Shanghai, and her work has been featured in the *New York Times*, *Wall Street Journal, Fast Company, Fortune*, and also on the BBC, CNN, and more.

YUDI ELA ECHEVARRIA is a photographer based between Los Angeles and New York City. She specializes in still life, portraiture, food & beverage, and fashion & beauty. A through-line of her work is the continued desire to explore the way light and materials interact with one another while, stylistically, evoking the mood of bygone eras and culture. She seeks to create imagery that have a quality of timelessness and reference vintage and antique moods, while staying grounded in contemporary life. Today, she experiments with blending these applications, using both digital and mechanical cameras to achieve similar results in her final images. In her work, she seeks to marry both past and present, the gauzy allure of dream worlds and immediacy of reality.

Acknowledgments

As anyone who has ever written a book of any kind can attest, this journey is a true labor of love and madness. To be honest, if I had known all that it entailed, I probably wouldn't have taken my first steps. But like all things worth pursuing, the road is treacherous but rewarding, and I couldn't have done it without the help of a village. I wrote this book during the most difficult and intense year of building Fly By Jing. Our rapid growth in the past four years has meant exponential demands on my team, our infrastructure, and my own accelerated growth as a leader. Completing this book on top of leading my company through its most critical junctures has taught me about the compression of time one can achieve through the force of sheer will, and the cost that comes with it. It's taught me about the interconnectedness of all things and that nothing happens in a vacuum. It's taught me to slow down, take time, savor each page and bite, and honor the process, not just the destination. Holding this book in my hands today, I feel humbled by the culmination of all those lessons and immense gratitude for everyone who was a part of this ride.

Four years ago, I couldn't have imagined that this sauce I cooked up in my small Shanghai kitchen would one day help to shape the way we eat in this country. To see our products on the shelves of Target and Whole Foods, and now these recipes from our humble supperclub beginnings out in the world, is a feeling only rivaled by the pride in seeing the rising tide of mission and vision-driven brands created by founders of color in the market today. This book is an important marker in our collective journeys, the documentation of what is possible from the seed of a dream, and the courage to reclaim one voice and one name. Our mission is to evolve culture through taste, and we are only getting started.

To my parents, who gave me life, love, wonder, adventure, the wild journey we embarked on together, and all the doors that opened along the way. Thank you for giving me the structure from which to build, and the safety from which to dream big.

To T, for helping me see in me what you see, for being my biggest cheerleader and forever rock.

To My team at FBJ, for your passion, dedication, and care. Thank you for taking a leap of faith in us. You are all bending reality and creating magic.

To Michele, without your guidance and encouragement this book would simply not exist. Thank you for believing in me, and for your patience and kind persistence.

To Kelly and Andrea, thank you for taking a chance on this book. Four years ago, the possibility of a book about chili crisp hitting the mainstream was a just faraway dream. Thank you for giving me the opportunity to expand more palates and minds.

To Claire and Lizzie, I have such appreciation for the master class you've both shown me in care and meticulousness. Thank you for your patience and for helping bring forward the best version of this book.

To Stacey, thank you for your friendship and partnership, your words are a direct translation of my soul.

To Yudi, Rebecca, and Caroline, your vision and genius are what makes this book pop. I set out to create a visual experience unlike anything you'd expect to see from a book about Chinese food, and you so masterfully brought it to life.

To all the founders, creators, dreamers, and doers out there, thank you for what you do, for what you sacrifice, for the value you create, and for not giving up. Through precession, your actions are changing the world.

Index

A

Aioli, Chili Crisp, 226
alcoholic beverages. *See* cocktails
almond butter
    Spicy Almond Butter Cookies, 194
almonds
    Spicy Almond Butter Cookies, 194
Ants Climbing Up a Tree, 120
avocados
    Chilled Tofu with Avocado, 54

B

bacon
    Wagyu Cheeseburger Pot Stickers, 87
Baijiu Negroni, 207
basil, Thai
    Sichuan Popcorn Chicken, 88
    Spicy Three-Cup Chicken, 116
bean sprouts
    Pickled Mustard Green Fish, 108
beef
    Dan Dan Noodles, 171
    Hot Pot, 136–37
    Mala Xiang Guo, 139
    Mapo Eggplant, 149
    Mapo Ragu with Hand-Pulled Noodles, 181
    Mapo Tofu, 104
    Tingly Beef Guokui, 91
    Wagyu Cheeseburger Pot Stickers, 87
Biang Biang Noodles, 178
    Mapo Ragu with Hand-Pulled Noodles, 181
Bingfen "Ice Jelly," 186
black beans, fermented, 27
    Twice-Cooked Pork, 128
black vinegar, 24
Bloody Sichuan Caesar, 208
bok choy, baby
    Mala Xiang Guo, 139
broccolini
    Sheet Pan Mala-Spiced Roast Chicken, 119
Brown Sugar Mochi, 190
Brussels sprouts
    Sheet Pan Zhong-Glazed Salmon, 111

C

cabbage
    Chili Crisp Vinaigrette Cabbage, 154
    Hongshao Carnitas Tacos, 124
    Sichuan Lacto-Fermented Pickles, 39–40

Cacio e Pepe, Sichuan, 174
caiziyou (Sichuan rapeseed oil), 23–24
Cake, Spiced Sticky Date, 198
Campari
    Baijiu Negroni, 207
Caramel Brittle, Fish Sauce, 193
carrots
    Sheet Pan Mala-Spiced Roast Chicken, 119
    Sichuan Lacto-Fermented Pickles, 39–40
cauliflower
    Mala Xiang Guo, 139
celtuce
    Celtuce, Vermicelli, and Chicken Salad, 41–42
    Celtuce in Tribute Pepper Oil, 45
Chaoshou, Chili Oil, 83
cheese
    Chili Paneer, 157
    Sichuan Cacio e Pepe, 174
    Wagyu Cheeseburger Pot Stickers, 87
Chengdu Scallion Pancakes, 61
Chengdu's food culture, 158
chicken
    Celtuce, Vermicelli, and Chicken Salad, 41–42
    Lazi Chicken Wings, 115
    Saliva Chicken, 62
    Sheet Pan Mala-Spiced Roast Chicken, 119
    Sichuan Popcorn Chicken, 88
    Spicy Three-Cup Chicken, 116
Chili Char Siu Pork Jowls, 131
chili crisp
    about, 14–15
    purchasing, 21
    Sichuan Chili Crisp, 220
    varieties, 14–15
Chili Crisp Aioli, 226
Chili Crisp Sundae with Fish Sauce
        Caramel Brittle, 193
Chili Crisp Vinaigrette, 226
    Chili Crisp Vinaigrette Cabbage, 154
    Chilled Tofu with Avocado, 54
Chili Furu Sauce, 228
Chili Oil, 219
    Chili Oil Chaoshou, 83
    Mapo Eggplant, 149
    Mapo Ragu with Hand-Pulled Noodles, 181
    Mapo Tofu, 104
    Spicy Scallion Oil Noodles, 177
    Strange-Flavor Sauce, 227
Chili Paneer, 157

chili peppers, dried
  about, 23
  erjingtiao, 23, 24
  Ground Chili Powder, 218
  Hot Pot, 136–37
  Kungpao Shrimp, 112
  Mala Simple Syrup, 211
  Sichuan Lacto-Fermented Pickles, 39–40
chili peppers, fresh
  Sichuan Lacto-Fermented Pickles, 39–40
  Sichuan XO Sauce, 225
Chili Powder, Ground, 218
chili sauce, pickled
  Fish-Fragrant Sauce, 228
chili sauces in other cultures, 15
Chilled Sesame Noodles, 168
Chilled Tofu with Avocado, 54
Chinese cuisine, 94–96
Chinese greens. *See* greens, Chinese
Chinese ingredients
  black vinegar, 24
  doubanjiang, 24–27
  dried chili peppers, 23
  dry spices, 28
  fermented black beans, 27
  furu (fermented tofu), 28
  pickled mustard greens, 28
  rock sugar, 28
  sesame oil, 27
  sesame paste, 27
  Sichuan chili crisp, 21
  Sichuan pepper, 21–23, 31
  Sichuan rapeseed oil, 23–24
  soy sauce, 24
  Yibin yacai, 27
Clamato juice
  Bloody Sichuan Caesar, 208
cocktails
  Baijiu Negroni, 207
  Bloody Sichuan Caesar, 208
  Mala Margarita, 212
  Sparkling Berry Shrub, 204
  Spicy Paloma, 211
Collagen Congee, 164
compound flavors (fuhewei), 31
condiments and seasonings
  Chili Crisp Aioli, 226
  Chili Crisp Vinaigrette, 226
  Chili Furu Sauce, 228

Chili Oil, 219
Fish-Fragrant Sauce, 228
Ginger-Scallion Chili Sauce, 228
Ground Chili Powder, 218
Ground Roasted Sichuan Pepper, 218
Kungpao Sauce, 225
Mala Spice Mix, 223
Salt and Sichuan Pepper Seasoning, 223
Sichuan Chili Crisp, 220
Sichuan Sweet Soy Sauce, 224
Sichuan XO Sauce, 225
Strange-Flavor Sauce, 227
Tribute Pepper Oil, 219
Zhong Sauce, 224
Zhong Sesame Dressing, 227
Congee, Collagen, 164
cookies
  Salt and Sichuan Pepper Walnut
    Cookies, 197
  Spicy Almond Butter Cookies, 194
Crudo, Yuzu Tribute Pepper, 50
cucumbers
  Chilled Sesame Noodles, 168
  Cucumber and Yuba Salad, 46

D

Dace Fried Rice, 167
daikon
  Sichuan Lacto-Fermented Pickles, 39–40
Dan Dan Noodles, 171
dashi
  Silky Steamed Eggs, 58
dates
  Spiced Sticky Date Cake, 198
desserts. *See* sweets
Deviled Tea Eggs, 57
Douban Fish, 107
doubanjiang, 24–27
  Douban Fish, 107
  Hot Pot, 136–37
  Mapo Tofu, 104
  Sichuan XO Sauce, 225
  Twice-Cooked Pork, 128
douchi (fermented black beans), 27
Douhua, Savory Soft, 144
dressings
  Chili Crisp Vinaigrette, 226
  Zhong Sesame Dressing, 227
drinks. *See* cocktails

dumplings. *See also* wontons
    Wagyu Cheeseburger Pot Stickers, 87
    Zhong Dumplings, 84

E
eggplant
    Fish-Fragrant Crispy Eggplant, 147
    Mapo Eggplant, 149
eggs
    Deviled Tea Eggs, 57
    Silky Steamed Eggs, 58
eggs, quail
    Hot Pot, 136–37
    Mala Xiang Guo, 139
erjingtiao dried chili peppers, 23, 24
    Hot and Sour Stir-Fried Potatoes, 146
    Lazi Chicken Wings, 115
    Mala Spice Mix, 223
    Pickled Mustard Green Fish, 108

F
fermented black beans, 27
fish and seafood
    Dace Fried Rice, 167
    Douban Fish, 107
    Hot Pot, 136–37
    Kungpao Shrimp, 112
    Mala Xiang Guo, 139
    Pickled Mustard Green Fish, 108
    Sheet Pan Zhong-Glazed Salmon, 111
    Sichuan XO Sauce, 225
    Strange-Flavor Poke, 53
    Yuzu Tribute Pepper Crudo, 50
Fish-Fragrant Crispy Eggplant, 147
Fish-Fragrant Sauce, 228
    Fish-Fragrant Crispy Eggplant (variation), 147
Fish Sauce Caramel Brittle, 193
    Chili Crisp Sundae with Fish Sauce
        Caramel Brittle, 193
flavor profiles
    compound flavors (fuhewei), 31
Fly By Jing, 9, 21, 64–71
fly restaurants, 158
Fried Rice, Dace, 167
fuhewei (compound flavors), 31
furu (fermented tofu), 28
    Chili Furu Sauce, 228

G
Gao, Jing ("Jenny"), 64–71
Ginger-Scallion Chili Sauce, 228
grapefruit juice
    Spicy Paloma, 211

greens, Chinese
    Hot Pot, 136–37
    Stir-Fried Chinese Greens, 153
Ground Chili Powder, 218
    Ginger-Scallion Chili Sauce, 228
    Sichuan Chili Crisp, 220
    Zhong Sauce, 224
Ground Roasted Sichuan Pepper, 218
    Chili Furu Sauce, 228
    Chili Oil, 219
    Sichuan Cacio e Pepe, 174
    Sichuan Chili Crisp, 220
    Strange-Flavor Sauce, 227
    Tribute Pepper Oil, 219
Guokui, Tingly Beef, 91

H
ham
    Sichuan XO Sauce, 225
hamachi
    Yuzu Tribute Pepper Crudo, 50
hierarchy of taste, 95–96
Hongshao Carnitas Tacos, 124
Hot and Sour Stir-Fried Potatoes, 146
Hot and Sour Sweet Potato Noodles, 175
hot pot
    about, 133
    Mala Xiang Guo, 139
    recipe, 136–37

I
ice cream
    Chili Crisp Sundae with Fish Sauce
        Caramel Brittle, 193
"Ice Jelly" (Bingfen), 186

K
kinako (roasted soybean powder)
    Brown Sugar Mochi, 190
konjac powder
    Bingfen "Ice Jelly," 186
Koshuiji (Saliva Chicken), 62
Kungpao Sauce, 225
    Kungpao Meatballs, 127
    Kungpao Shrimp, 112

L
Lazi Chicken Wings, 115
leeks
    Leek, Tofu, and Peanut Salad, 49
    Twice-Cooked Pork, 128
Liangfen Jelly Noodles, 80

lotus root
    Mala Lotus Root Chips, 79
    Mala Xiang Guo, 139

M

Mala Margarita, 212
Mala Simple Syrup, 211
    Mala Margarita, 212
    Spicy Paloma, 211
Mala Spice Mix, 223
    Lazi Chicken Wings, 115
    Mala Lotus Root Chips, 79
    Mala Margarita, 212
    Mala-Spiced Smashed Potatoes, 150
    Sheet Pan Mala-Spiced Roast Chicken, 119
Mala Xiang Guo, 139
Mapo Eggplant, 149
Mapo Ragu with Hand-Pulled Noodles, 181
Mapo Tofu, 104
Margarita, Mala, 212
mayonnaise
    Chili Crisp Aioli, 226
Meatballs, Kungpao, 127
mezcal
    Mala Margarita, 212
    Spicy Paloma, 211
Mochi, Brown Sugar, 190
mung bean starch
    Liangfen Jelly Noodles, 80
mushrooms
    Hot Pot, 136–37
    Mala Xiang Guo, 139
mustard greens, pickled, 28
Musubi, Zhong Spam, 92

N

Negroni, Baijiu, 207
noodles
    Ants Climbing Up a Tree, 120
    Biang Biang Noodles, 178
    Celtuce, Vermicelli, and Chicken Salad, 41–42
    Chilled Sesame Noodles, 168
    Dan Dan Noodles, 171
    Hot and Sour Sweet Potato Noodles, 175
    Hot Pot, 136–37
    Liangfen Jelly Noodles, 80
    Mapo Ragu with Hand-Pulled Noodles, 181
    Pickled Mustard Green Fish, 108
    Sichuan Cacio e Pepe, 174
    Spicy Scallion Oil Noodles, 177
    Sweet Water Noodles, 172
nori. *See also* seaweed
    Zhong Spam Musubi, 92

O

oil(s)
    Chili Oil, 219
    sesame oil, 27
    Sichuan rapeseed oil, 23–24
    Tribute Pepper Oil, 219
orange liqueur
    Mala Margarita, 212

P

Paloma, Spicy, 211
Paneer, Chili, 157
peanuts
    Fish Sauce Caramel Brittle, 193
    Leek, Tofu, and Peanut Salad, 49
    Savory Soft Douhua, 144
pears
    Poached Pears in Sichuan Pepper Syrup, 189
pepper, Sichuan, 21–23, 31
Pickled Chili Pineapples, 124
    Hongshao Carnitas Tacos, 124
pickled chili sauce
    Fish-Fragrant Sauce, 228
pickled mustard greens (suancai), 28
    Pickled Mustard Green Fish, 108
Pickled Red Onions, 53
Pickles, Sichuan Lacto-Fermented, 39–40
pineapple
    Pickled Chili Pineapples, 124
Poached Pears in Sichuan Pepper Syrup, 189
poke
    Strange-Flavor Poke, 53
Popcorn Chicken, Sichuan, 88
pork
    Ants Climbing Up a Tree, 120
    Chili Char Siu Pork Jowls, 131
    Chili Oil Chaoshou, 83
    Hongshao Carnitas Tacos, 124
    Hot Pot, 136–37
    Kungpao Meatballs, 127
    Red-Braised Pork Belly, 123
    Twice-Cooked Pork, 128
    Zhong Dumplings, 84

nuts
    Fish Sauce Caramel Brittle, 193
    Kungpao Shrimp, 112
    Leek, Tofu, and Peanut Salad, 49
    Salt and Sichuan Pepper Walnut Cookies, 197
    Savory Soft Douhua, 144
    Spicy Almond Butter Cookies, 194
    Strange-Flavor Mixed Nuts, 76

potatoes
    Hot and Sour Stir-Fried Potatoes, 146
    Mala-Spiced Smashed Potatoes, 150
    Mala Xiang Guo, 139
    Sheet Pan Mala-Spiced Roast Chicken, 119
pot stickers
    Wagyu Cheeseburger Pot Stickers, 87

Q

quail eggs. *See* eggs, quail

R

rapeseed oil, Sichuan, 23–24
Red-Braised Pork Belly, 123
    Hongshao Carnitas Tacos, 124
Red Onions, Pickled, 53
"red rabbit," 41
rice
    Collagen Congee, 164
    Dace Fried Rice, 167
    Zhong Spam Musubi, 92
rice flour
    Brown Sugar Mochi, 190
rice vinegar
    Sparkling Berry Shrub, 204
rock sugar, 28

S

salads
    Celtuce, Vermicelli, and Chicken
        Salad, 41–42
    Cucumber and Yuba Salad, 46
    Leek, Tofu, and Peanut Salad, 49
Saliva Chicken, 62
salmon
    Sheet Pan Zhong-Glazed Salmon, 111
Salt and Sichuan Pepper Seasoning, 223
    Bloody Sichuan Caesar, 208
Salt and Sichuan Pepper Walnut
        Cookies, 197
sauces. *See* condiments and seasonings
Savory Soft Douhua, 144
scallions
    Chengdu Scallion Pancakes, 61
    Dace Fried Rice, 167
    Ginger-Scallion Chili Sauce, 228
    Spicy Scallion Oil Noodles, 177
scallops, dried
    Sichuan XO Sauce, 225
seasonings. *See* condiments and seasonings
seaweed. *See also* nori
    Hot Pot, 136–37
Sesame Noodles, Chilled, 168

sesame oil, 27
sesame paste, 27
    Chili Furu Sauce, 228
    Strange-Flavor Sauce, 227
    Zhong Sesame Dressing, 227
Shangxing Liangfen (Liangfen Jelly Noodles), 80
Shaoxing wine
    Hot Pot, 136–37
    Red-Braised Pork Belly, 123
    Spicy Three-Cup Chicken, 116
Sheet Pan Mala-Spiced Roast Chicken, 119
Sheet Pan Zhong-Glazed Salmon, 111
shrimp
    Kungpao Shrimp, 112
    Mala Xiang Guo, 139
shrimp, dried
    Sichuan XO Sauce, 225
Shrub, Sparkling Berry, 204
Sichuan Cacio e Pepe, 174
Sichuan Chili Crisp, 220
    about, 14–15, 21
    Chili Crisp Aioli, 226
    Chili Crisp Sundae with Fish Sauce
        Caramel Brittle, 193
    Chili Crisp Vinaigrette, 226
Sichuan Lacto-Fermented Pickles, 39–40
    Bloody Sichuan Caesar, 208
Sichuan pepper, 21–23, 31
    Ground Roasted Sichuan Pepper, 218
    Salt and Sichuan Pepper Seasoning, 223
Sichuan Popcorn Chicken, 88
Sichuan Province, 30–31
Sichuan rapeseed oil, 23–24
    Hot Pot, 136–37
    Sichuan Chili Crisp, 220
    Sichuan XO Sauce, 225
Sichuan Sweet Soy Sauce, 224
    Zhong Sauce, 224
Sichuan XO Sauce, 225
Silky Steamed Eggs, 58
Simple Syrup, Mala, 211
soy sauce
    about, 24
    Chili Furu Sauce, 228
    Sichuan Sweet Soy Sauce, 224
Spam
    Zhong Spam Musubi, 92
Sparkling Berry Shrub, 204
Spiced Sticky Date Cake, 198
spices, dried, 28
Spicy Almond Butter Cookies, 194
Spicy Paloma, 211
Spicy Scallion Oil Noodles, 177

Spicy Three-Cup Chicken, 116
Stir-Fried Chinese Greens, 153
Strange-Flavor Mixed Nuts, 76
Strange-Flavor Sauce, 227
    Strange-Flavor Poke, 53
string beans, long
    Sichuan Lacto-Fermented Pickles, 39–40
suancai (pickled mustard greens), 28
sugar, rock, 28
Sweet Potato Noodles, Hot and Sour, 175
sweets
    Bingfen "Ice Jelly," 186
    Brown Sugar Mochi, 190
    Chili Crisp Sundae with Fish Sauce
        Caramel Brittle, 193
    Poached Pears in Sichuan Pepper Syrup, 189
    Salt and Sichuan Pepper Walnut
        Cookies, 197
    Spiced Sticky Date Cake, 198
    Spicy Almond Butter Cookies, 194
Sweet Water Noodles, 172
Swiss chard
    Collagen Congee, 164

T
Tacos, Hongshao Carnitas, 124
tallow, beef
    Hot Pot, 136–37
tapioca starch
    Sichuan Popcorn Chicken, 88
tea
    Deviled Tea Eggs, 57
Thai basil. See basil, Thai
Three-Cup Chicken, Spicy, 116
tianmianjiang
    Twice-Cooked Pork, 128
Tingly Beef Guokui, 91
tofu
    Chilled Tofu with Avocado, 54
    Douban Fish, 107
    furu (fermented tofu), 28
    Hot Pot, 136–37
    Leek, Tofu, and Peanut Salad, 49
    Mala Xiang Guo, 139
    Mapo Tofu, 104
    Savory Soft Douhua, 144
tortillas, corn
    Hongshao Carnitas Tacos, 124
tribute pepper. See Sichuan pepper
Tribute Pepper Oil, 219
    Celtuce in Tribute Pepper Oil, 45
    Yuzu Tribute Pepper Crudo, 50
Twice-Cooked Pork, 128

V
vegetables. See also specific kinds
    Hot Pot, 136–37
vermicelli
    Ants Climbing Up a Tree, 120
    Celtuce, Vermicelli, and Chicken Salad, 41–42
    Pickled Mustard Green Fish, 108
vermouth, sweet
    Baijiu Negroni, 207
Vinaigrette, Chili Crisp, 226
vinegar, black, 24
vodka
    Bloody Sichuan Caesar, 208

W
Wagyu Cheeseburger Pot Stickers, 87
walnuts
    Salt and Sichuan Pepper Walnut
        Cookies, 197
waxberries
    Sparkling Berry Shrub, 204
whiskey
    Spiced Sticky Date Cake, 198
wontons. See also dumplings
    Chili Oil Chaoshou, 83

X
XO Sauce, Sichuan, 225

Y
Yibin yacai, 27
    Dan Dan Noodles, 171
yuba
    Cucumber and Yuba Salad, 46
    Hot Pot, 136–37
    Mala Xiang Guo, 139
yuzu ponzu
    Yuzu Tribute Pepper Crudo, 50

Z
Zhong Dumplings, 84
Zhong Sauce, 224
    Saliva Chicken, 62
    Sheet Pan Zhong-Glazed Salmon, 111
    Zhong Sesame Dressing, 227
    Zhong Spam Musubi, 92
Zhong Sesame Dressing, 227
    Sweet Water Noodles, 172

Typefaces: Linotype's Helvetica, Carvalho Bernau's Jean-Luc, and Commercial
Type's Publico

Library of Congress Cataloging-in-Publication Data

Names: Gao, Jing, 1987- author. | Echevarria, Yudi Ela, photographer.
Title: The book of Sichuan chili crisp : spicy recipes and stories from Fly
    by Jing's Kitchen / Jing Gao, founder of Fly by Jing ; photography by
    Yudi Ela Echevarria.
Description: California : Ten Speed Press, [2023] | Includes index. |
    Summary: "In Jing Gao's first cookbook, she shows you that nearly every dish
    can be elevated with Sichuan flavors and invites you to explore the "not
    traditional but personal" flavors of Fly By Jing's savory, spicy chili crisp through
    85 hot recipes for everything from drinks to dessert"-- Provided by
    publisher.
Identifiers: LCCN 2022055292 (print) | LCCN 2022055293 (ebook) | ISBN
    9781984862174 (hardcover) | ISBN 9781984862181 (ebook)
Subjects: LCSH: Cooking, Chinese--Szechwan style. | Cooking (Hot pepper
    sauces) | LCGFT: Cookbooks.
Classification: LCC TX724.5.C5 G35 2023 (print) | LCC TX724.5.C5 (ebook)
    | DDC 641.5951/38--dc23/eng/20221122
LC record available at https://lccn.loc.gov/2022055292
LC ebook record available at https://lccn.loc.gov/2022055293

Hardcover ISBN: 978-1-9848-6217-4
eBook ISBN: 978-1-9848-6218-1

Printed in China

Acquiring editor: Kelly Snowden | Project editor: Claire Yee
Production editor: Ashley Pierce
Designer: Lizzie Allen | Production designers: Mari Gill and Faith Hague
Production manager: Serena Sigona | Prepress color manager: Nick Patton
Food stylist: Caroline Hwang | Prop stylist: Rebecca Bartoshesky
Copyeditor: Dolores York | Proofreader: Sasha Tropp | Indexer: Amy Hall
Publicist: David Hawk | Marketer: Monica Stanton

10 9 8 7 6 5 4 3 2 1

First Edition